STOP LIVING PAY TO PAY

ISBN 9781925995213

Published in Australia and New Zealand by

Booktopia Editions, an imprint of Booktopia Pty Ltd

Unit E1, 3-29 Birnie Avenue, Lidcombe, NSW 2141, Australia

Printed and bound in Australia by Ligare

The paper this book is printed on is in accordance with the standards of the Forest Stewardship Council®. The FSC® promotes environmentally responsible, socially beneficial and economically viable management of the world's forests.

booktopia.com.au

How to Break the Cycle of Toxic Debt

STOP LIVING PAY TO PAY

GREG SMITH

CONTENTS

FOREWORD

This is not your normal how-to money book.

It is based on real-life experiences over the past thirty years from my personal life and my life as a financial industry professional.

I have all the undergraduate and post graduate qualifications anyone could wish for, plus more financial services qualifications than you can poke a stick at. But one qualification I was not expecting was when I joined the pay-to-pay cycle club.

I managed to get myself out of that club but I can tell you, when I was in it, everything – and I mean everything – seemed to go wrong. This book tells you how I got out of it and how you can too – more easily than you may think.

Falling into the pay-to-pay cycle is something that happens to many Australians every day. Since the COVID-19 crisis close to 5.9 million Australians have fallen into the cycle due to job losses and the general economic downturn, many for the first time in their lives. For others this is a recurring pattern. The hardest thing is to find your way out when you feel yourself spiralling (sometimes silently) out of control. That's where I will help you.

You'll discover how to build up a stack of knowledge that will give you the confidence to approach money in a way you never thought possible.

My tried-and-tested techniques will enable you to take control of your finances and connect the big picture with your day-to-day life.

INTRODUCTION

Before we jump in, I thought I'd give you some context – who I am, how I landed in the pay-to-pay cycle and how I managed to get out. It feels weird and a bit overindulgent to be writing this, but please bear with me as it will set the scene for the rest of the book.

When I reflect on my life over the past thirty years, I must say it has been one hell of a roller-coaster. There have been times when everything I touched turned to gold, and then other times when my world crumbled physically, emotionally and financially.

In that time I've worked for some amazing companies, been made redundant, got married and divorced, built up a successful management consultancy, made a lot of money, published seventeen books, launched a world-first money centre, been struck down by a mystery illness, lost the sight in one eye, lost my money (and I mean lost it all!), been left at the altar, watched my money slip away again, as a business venture came crashing down. Got hit with another set of health setbacks, found love and had two wonderful boys.

Not much really! But tell you what, all these experiences have taught me some unbelievably valuable lessons, and for that I believe I'm a better person. These things have a way of affecting every aspect of your life. I know they did with me, especially my finances. Without my health I couldn't work, without a job I had no income and without love I didn't have the support to give me the strength I needed to take risks.

I like to call these setbacks "Money Monsters", as they have a way of creeping up and scaring the living daylights out of you. Sometimes you get a real fright, and at other times you just put them back in the cupboard where they belong and get on with life.

Depending on how you approach these Money Monsters determines how well you respond to any kind of financial setback. If you let them get the better of you, it could take you many years to recover, but if you attack the problem early, then things will quickly start to turn around and you will break out of the pay-to-pay cycle sooner.

One of the major lessons I've learned from this past two decades is that you need a great support network around you when things look like they are turning to dust.

Having a supportive family is a great, if you have that, but there are a number of other people out there who can, and will, help you. There's no point in putting your head in the sand and hoping a problem will go away (it definitely won't in the financial world, you can bank on that), so always, and I say that again, always ask for help.

'How you approach these Money Monsters determines how well you respond to setbacks.'

There will be many possible solutions to your problems, and someone will know someone or something to get you through. In my case, I was lucky to be well-connected and had a great family to provide me with the support I needed to get back on track.

The real energy, however, must come from you. No matter what situation you find yourself in, be it financial, physical, or emotional, you are the one who must find the will to go on. Others can give you support and guidance, but the will has to come from within. Let me give you a snapshot of some of the things that have happened to me over the last decade to explain what I mean.

Over the years I have been made redundant on a few occasions.

At one stage I held what I thought was a very stable job at a bank. It paid well, and I had just been given a pay rise following my annual review. But with one telephone call it was all over.. One minute I had a job, the next I was unemployed. It was such a crushing blow to my confidence. I'll never forget having to take the train home in the middle of the morning. Weird.

That really rocked my world and was a crushing blow to my confidence. I even found myself looking at jobs that paid a much lower salary than my previous position. But I had bills to pay, and so I looked at everything. I must say, after each redundancy a little piece of you dies. It sounds dramatic, but I really lost my way and convinced myself that I was unemployable. Mentally it was tough. Despite multiple attempts I simply couldn't land a job. So one day I woke up and thought "bugger it", if no one will have me I'll set up a business of my own. So I set up my consultancy, well away from the safety of corporate land.

'In these uncertain COVID-19 times you need to look at every angle to either find a job or create something of your own.'

Sure, the cash flow issues of a new business were tricky, but I was lucky enough to have good financial management skills so the transition was a little easier, and I had a bit of money stashed away to cover me during the hardest months. (A valuable lesson we'll learn later in this book!) It was tough going at first, as I must have heard "no" a million times. So often I wanted to give up. But once I landed my first contract my confidence increased at an exponential rate. It is amazing how self-redeeming it feels when you get paid for something you created. Over the next few years of hard work, I built up a profitable business that generated a great living.

Unfortunately, a few years later I was hit by health problems. A good work–life balance might be one of the keys to good health, but sixteen-hour days are clearly not! One minute I thought I was fighting fit, the next I was unconscious being rushed to hospital in an ambulance. Not once but four times in the space of three months! Add to this, I had my business spread across a number of areas and had to watch helplessly as each one of them crumbled while I was in and out of hospital.

Consequently, I lost that business and it cost me most of my money. Luckily, I had income protection insurance, which helped pay my personal daily living expenses while I got back on my feet. While I was recovering I had a lot of time to reset my goals in preparation for restarting my life. This included making a number of changes to the way I lived (diet and exercise), plus a significant refocus on how many hours I work a day and what business I expended my energy on.

I decided to set up my own financial services company focusing on finance broking, money coaching and financial planning. However, first I needed to undertake a training course to regain my qualifications, which was going to take 12 months to complete. The road seemed so long!

Even though I had the income protection insurance payments, they were only just covering my expenses. So I returned to being a marketing consultant to generate the all-important cash flow. The energy to do this had to come from within, but I wanted to have a better life and not live from pay-to-pay.

Before I move on, I must emphasise that you should never take your health for granted. The saying, "You don't know what you've got until it's gone", rings all so true when you lose your health. It affects every part of your life, and most of all your capacity to earn an income. Your health is your wealth – never forget it.

When it comes to relationships, I've just about seen it all. I've had some good ones and I've had some shockers. Talk about the proverbial rollercoaster of love. In 1990, I married my high school sweetheart and we set about building a life together. However, like thousands of Australian marriages, mine ended in divorce. It took its toll emotionally and halved my total worth overnight.

Luckily, we didn't have kids otherwise the outcome could have been extremely different, but it still hurt and took a while for me to recover emotionally. A number of years later I met another lady; we lived together for about five years and then decided to get married. Unfortunately, a few months prior to the wedding, she did a runner. I couldn't believe my luck. Here I was getting back on top financially and with my health. And whammo!

You wouldn't read about it!

Again, this had a massive impact on my finances. How? I had to replace all the household items my ex decided to take with her when she left. She pretty much cleaned out the house.

To clear my head, I decided to spoil myself (we all need to do this from time to time). I booked myself a ticket to Europe for a quick holiday and spent about $15,000. It was an expensive trip, but it felt like the best $15,000 I've ever spent.

Both relationship bust-ups affected my finances and emotions quite significantly, with most of the expenditure coming out of an emotional response. While there's no problem dealing with emotions in this way, the lesson was not to let my emotions go overboard and disguise a deeper problem with retail therapy. In other words, I shouldn't have spent the $15,000 – a simple road trip up the coast would have had the same impact.

Clearly, emotions and money can be a lethal cocktail and the trick is keeping both in check. That's why in Chapter 1, I discuss what I call Money Personalities and show you how to discover and harness them, regardless of your emotional state.

'Emotions and money can be a lethal cocktail and the trick is keeping both in check.'

By now you may be wondering to yourself if my life gets any better. On the whole it does but there are always are highs and lows.

After I retrained, I established my financial services company and built that up to a solid business, which I sold late 2008 just before the global financial crisis. I then met a wonderful woman, who is now my partner, and we have two beautiful boys. On the downside, however, my return to corporate life for a few years was a real low, as the redundancy Money Monster kept following me around.

Clearly the universe wasn't whispering; it was screaming at me to do my own thing. And that I did. Now I have multiple interests in multiple companies across many industries.

Sure, the impact of COVID-19 has affected me like everyone else. I have seen a massive drop in my income and savings, but because I am now working much smarter and have set up many different sources of passive, income I'll be able to keep those Money Monsters away. But they are always out there, and you never know when they might strike!

Having been in and out of the pay-to-pay cycle over the past thirty years has really taught me the hard lessons. That's why I hope you will read this book carefully and pay attention to all of the tips and techniques. They will help you break out of the living from pay-to-pay cycle.

ABOUT ME

In the introduction section I introduced the concept of Money Monsters and laid out my life over the last thirty years. Now my publisher wants me to connect with you and give you a bit of a history lesson going back to my birth.

You are most welcome to skip this bit. But everyone has a story, and this is mine.

I grew up in Richmond in NSW on a small thirty-hectare farm. Right in the middle of the property were three houses, all within fifty metres of each other. (It was cheaper to build them that way!) I lived in the first house with Mum, Dad and my brothers. Mum's sister and her husband were in the middle house and my maternal grandparents lived in the third.

Life on the farm was often a bit like a fairy-tale. I had all my family in one spot, plus a big area to explore, which kept me more than adequately occupied. Having my family so close, I was learning from them pretty much on a daily basis. My aunty, uncle and grandparents were all post–World War II refugees from Eastern Europe, and I got to discover their views on everything from culture and politics to work ethic and money. Dad, a fifth generation Australian and the only non-European, brought an interesting flavour to the mix. I learned a great deal from him, especially his entrepreneurial skills.

My two brothers were great fun to grow up with. My younger brother, who will always be my little brother (he's now in his late forties with kids), was a constant source of entertainment, and my older brother was someone I always looked up to. Although occasionally we tried to kill each other!

School was not exactly the most enjoyable period of my life as I didn't like the dogmatic style of teaching and the capital punishment that was dished out.

At school, I had a small but tight group of friends. We would constantly talk money and finance, whether it be business, investment, property or the share market, and we'd always be debating some sort of economic or political policy. Kind of daggy, I guess. Perhaps that's why I only had a small group of friends!

At university I studied (you guessed it) economics. Despite my best efforts to resist the temptations of the university social club, I found myself at the end of the first year seriously failing (can't explain it – perhaps it was all that new-found freedom after those draconian schooling years). To hedge my bets (I always like to protect my downside risk!) I looked in the paper for a job. Long story short, I landed a job at the Australian Stock Exchange (the Sydney Stock Exchange in those days) as a Financial Analyst. Fancy title, but in reality I was a glorified proofreader. I've got to say the Stock Exchange changed my life. Not only did I meet my boss, who gave me a whole new perspective on money, it also taught me how knowledge is fundamental to successful money management and investment. Speaking of knowledge, I continued at university part-time; my grades went up and I graduated with Distinction. See what happens when you have a purpose.

After more than ten years at the Stock Exchange, I jumped ship and went into banking. I also wrote my first book called Do It Yourself Marketing. I did this for two reasons. The first was to share the knowledge I had accumulated by working at the Stock Exchange and gain more credibility. The second was, I wanted a passive income stream over and above my salary. I had a mortgage to pay and investments to build. And let's face it, a single source of income is just not enough.

'The Stock Exchange changed my life: I could see how knowledge is fundamental to success.'

My few years in banking ended pretty abruptly when I was made redundant. Then I took a job in advertising. It was a real eye-opener and I only stayed a short time; about the third month into it I had a blinding flash that I should be doing it for myself. I followed my instinct and set up my own consultancy.

When I was working for myself, a great number of opportunities seemed to magically come my way; I don't know if it was good fortune or good measure (a combination of both I suspect), but I found myself consulting to the banking industry and the investment industry, working with a number of great firms in other sectors and building a good business.

My move back into the money world came about when I wrote a book called More For Less back in the late nineties, which was a simple guide to saving money on everyday things. As a stroke of luck, this book somehow made it across the Deputy Editor's desk at Woman's Day magazine and she called me up and asked me to be the money editor. I was thrilled to have this opportunity to communicate with millions of readers each week and help them with their money situation. I did that for more than seven years.

A number of radio stations around Australia then contacted me to have a chat to them on a regular basis about money events and how they affect the average person's hip pocket. One radio station (2UE in Sydney) even gave me a one-hour money show which led to a regular half-hour on a prime-time radio program on the same network. Radio led to a regional TV spot with NBN Television for three years, then onto Channel 10. All of these media activities enabled me to use my gift for communicating about the complex world of money in simple English, which I totally love.

In the early 2000s, I found myself writing a weekly page for The Daily Telegraph's Money and You Section. From these media outlets I received a huge number of visitors to my website from this media exposure, with the most common question being "Why do I do what I do with my money?" That's why in 2002, I wrote a book called Unlock the Secrets of Your Money Personality.

Just when I thought I was indestructible, I got involved in a retail/dotcom venture called the Money Café a world's first money and finance centre. Unfortunately, for many reasons, it failed, leaving me high and dry financially – a nice way to say "screwed", I guess. After trading out of this mess (you'll see how I did it later), I picked myself up, set up my financial services company, then went back into corporate land only to get made redundant a few times.

Now I am once again working for myself, with multiple interests in multiple companies across many industries. Plus, after a little over ten years, I'm back at Woman's Day magazine and on radio helping Australians control their money.

Well, there you have it, my life in about 1,200 words – the story of a passionate, empathetic entrepreneur with a burning desire to help others learn more about their money so they don't have to live from pay-to-pay and can enjoy life to the fullest.

ONE MORE THING

A good mate of mine called me, depressed and in a panic, a few days before I finished writing this book. He hadn't lost his job or had a pay cut as a result of COVID-19. What had happened was he had bitten off more than he could chew.

Late in 2019 he had bought a new house at the top of the market and mortgaged himself up to the eyeballs. Not only that, he had a personal loan that never seemed to end and a maxed-out credit card for which he could barely cover the minimum monthly repayments. In his own words his income was being smothered by his expenses.

Just like anyone in his situation he tried to find extra cash, but unfortunately that proved fruitless; he just couldn't see how he could cut back any more. To meet him on the street you'd think that he was quite a successful person. He had a good job, nice house, went on a few holidays a year with the kids, drove a nice car and had all the trappings. The only problem was, he was literally living from pay-to-pay with no savings whatsoever to cover him for emergencies.

When I told him I was just about to finish my book called How to Stop Living from Pay to Pay he almost jumped down the phone. He wanted it right then and there. Funny, that's the same reaction I've been getting from everyone I mention the name of this book to. It seems that my mate is not alone. It seems a common theme coming from all the emails I receive from my articles and radio segments are anything to go by.

With the financial devastation COVID-19 has left on Australia, our unemployment rate will probably top out at 10 per cent of the workforce over the coming year. Add to this the underemployment rate of a further 5–10 per cent (people who have had their hours reduced to three or four days a week), and the aggregate figure could end up closer to 15–20 per cent (well in excess of the Great Depression levels of the 1930s). That said there is a proverbial debt cliff about to hit Australia once the full effects of lost or lowered income becomes a reality. There is a real risk of a blow-out in mortgage, personal loan and credit card defaults, as 46 per cent of the Australian adult population stand to fall into the pay-to-pay cycle.

'Don't think for a moment that living from pay to pay is restricted to those on a low income.'

No matter the size of your income, it's what you do with it that counts. Don't think for a moment that living from pay to pay is restricted to those on a low income. Just look at my mate as a perfect example.

I fear that a financial tsunami is coming, as the financial fall out from COVID-19 is yet to be seen globally. It will affect us terribly (you'll see what I mean in Chapter 1). That's why it is ever so important you read this book. Let me ask, which would you prefer? To be in the pay-to-pay cycle when the financial tsunami hits, or well and truly out of the cycle and ready to face what it brings? I hope you choose the latter.

Now, let's find out how to stop living from pay to pay.

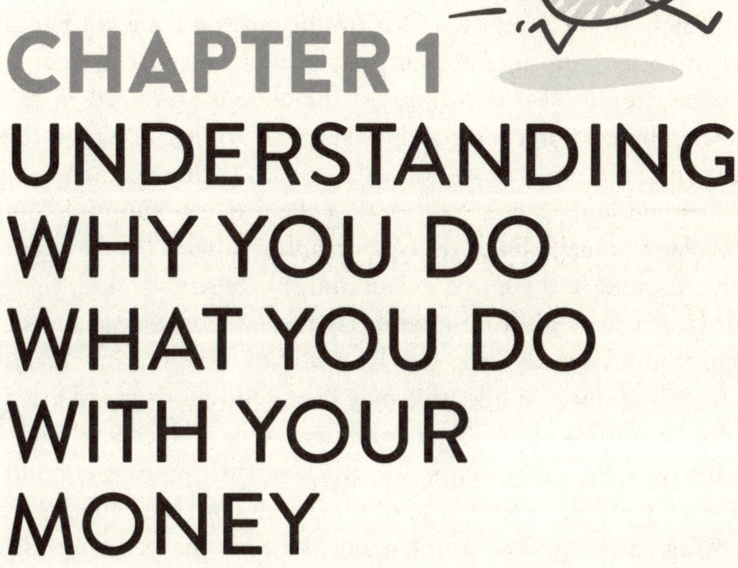

CHAPTER 1
UNDERSTANDING WHY YOU DO WHAT YOU DO WITH YOUR MONEY

What you are about to read will probably change the way you handle money forever.

In fact, if the following techniques have the same impact on you as they did on me, I can guarantee your money world will improve many times over.

But before we begin, I'd like you to answer a simple question? How badly do you really want to break out of the pay-to-pay cycle?

Think about this for a moment as there's a big difference between **needing** to break out of the pay-to-pay cycle and **wanting** to.

Believe it or not, the answer lies in the definition of needs and wants. For example, a **need** is something that has to be satisfied. It is generally non-emotional and short-term in nature.

A **want**, on the other hand, is much more of an emotional response that's directly connected to some sort of internal desire to make a change (be it for the short-term or long-term).

When it comes to breaking out of the pay-to-pay cycle you must start with a deep-down desire to make a change to your current world – a real want.

From here, you must make an emotional and behavioural commitment to breaking free (that means putting your heart into it). Then, when you need to, put in place actions that are going to generate results. I'll show you all the actions you need in the following chapters, but for now let's keep on drilling down on the fundamental reasons why you do what you do with your money.

When you look at it, a great deal of the way you approach and handle your money comes from your upbringing (I'll talk about this in a minute) and your conscious and subconscious mind.

When it comes to dealing with day-to-day money issues, your conscious mind usually takes over as it tries to solve as many issues as it can all at once. Whilst this may be a good momentary fix, it may not be addressing the bigger or longer-term problems.

Unfortunately, many people are stuck in their conscious mind and have big problems letting go of the day to day. They only focus on cutting costs and don't think about the steps they need to take to break the cycle.

Your subconscious is where the action is. Therefore you need to spend some quality time looking for potential reasons why you are being held back. It may be your upbringing; you grew up in a household that struggled for money and had an "I can't be rich" attitude. Alternatively, you may have the knowledge but lack the confidence to implement the necessary changes to break free. Of course, it could be you are just downright lazy.

All reasons aside, it is about wanting to make a change and making the emotional commitment to break free. Everyone in the pay-to-pay cycle needs to get out of it, however success belongs to those who are willing to make a concerted effort to do it. That's why you have to want to change. And that's why you have to understand that your subconscious is the key driver. Make the changes there and you're away.

Some of the changes you need to make will be painful (let me tell you, I know – been there, done that, I've even got the T-shirt!) and will probably take you out of your comfort zone.

To use an old cliché, it's all about "no pain, no gain", just like starting a fitness regime. Those first few times make you feel so sick you really want to give up, but if you stick at it and have a positive attitude (believe you can do it) you start feeling great and the results begin to show.

Unfortunately, neither I nor anyone else has a magic wand to make your life better overnight. It's going to take a bit of commitment from you and a few tools and techniques from me, so you can make the necessary improvements yourself. I'll share with you these tools and techniques shortly, but now let's look at the reasons why you are in the pay-to-pay cycle.

HOW DID YOU GET INTO THE LIVING FROM PAY-TO-PAY CYCLE?

There are many reasons why you can easily fall into the vicious pay-to-pay cycle in addition to your conscious and subconscious going into overdrive. In fact, some of the factors that lead us into the spiral are even more sinister, such as those I call Money Monsters. (I mentioned these in the introduction and will talk about how to avoid them in Chapter 7.) These come in different forms like losing your job, the fallout from a relationship breakup, an illness or accident, the birth of a new child, and so on. As you can imagine, each can – and often does – have a massive impact on your finances (plus your attitude to money) sending you into a real spin.

Other reasons why you might fall into the pay-to-pay cycle can in fact be self-inflicted. (Again I talk about these in Chapter 7, where I mention the Seven Deadly Money Sins!) In other words, you may have fallen victim to what I call the "got to have it now" bug. (I love giving names to things – it helps you relate to intangible concepts.)

This bug is a direct result of the buoyant economic times we have experienced over the past twenty-odd years (pre-COVID-19). As a result, we have all been spending more and more. To compound the problem, we are all living in a "got to have it now" society, which means rather than save up for things (like past generations did) we simply rack it up on the credit card or lock ourselves into "buy now, pay later" deals.

Sure, the temptations to spend are quite significant, and the pressures of keeping up with friends and family to have the latest and greatest are intensifying, but this is contributing to the racking up of significant debt. As a result, we as a nation are spending more than we earn. This is evidenced by an almost zero savings ratio (that is the percentage of savings to our income). On top of this, our expenditure ratio (the amount of money we spend as a percentage of our income) is currently close to 200 per cent and growing (most of this is going to service debt, be it mortgages or credit cards.

'Chances are you may have fallen victim to the dreaded 'got-to-have-it-now' bug.'

What this means is, for every $100 we earn we spend $200. Oh yes, you read it right! And this ratio has been growing steadily over the past five years. Unfortunately, debts have grown almost exponentially, however incomes have not maintained the same growth.

So, where are we getting the money from? I'll give you two guesses – credit cards and "buy now, pay later" schemes. According to the Reserve Bank of Australia, in March 2020 there was about $29 billion owing on the 14 million credit cards on issue.

Of that $29 billion, $7 billion is paid back in full each month. However, that leaves $19 billion left attracting interest at rates ranging from 9–19 per cent per annum. Add to this the exponential growth of buy now, pay later schemes and you get the picture. Credit card usage has fallen over recent years with the rise of the buy now, pay later companies such as Afterpay, Zip and Klarna, but with 66 percent of credit cards not paid off it is a serious concern. Credit card companies, on the other hand, love it and that's why so many people fall into the pay-to-pay cycle. To give you an example, let's say you have the average Australian credit card balance of

$3,231 and your interest rate is 11 per cent. If you only paid the minimum amount back each month it would take a whopping 14 years 6 months to pay it back and you'd end up paying back a total of $5,431! The credit card debt cycle is vicious.

BREAKING THE PAY-TO-PAY CYCLE: LEARNING FROM YOUR PAST

I've spoken about ways you may have fallen into the living from pay-to-pay cycle. Now, let me take you take a few steps back and look at some of the factors that influence the way you approach and handle money.

Before leaping into setting your goals and budgets, and all that good stuff, I'm going to get you to have a serious look at the key people in your life and the events that have influenced and shaped your current attitudes and approach to money. Why? I believe that you need to look deep into these influences to establish the reasons you do what you do with your money. Once you've got this information, I'll give you a few techniques to help you make the necessary changes to break out of the pay-to-pay cycle.

Okay, let's go.

Using the following template*, write down the key people in your life (one per row). For example, your mum, dad, uncle, aunty, brother, sister, best friend, work colleague.

Now write down what they taught you about money (list the good and bad things), when they taught you, what impact that had on you and, in the last column, whether you think that person had an overall positive or negative effect on your approach to money today.

THE KEY PEOPLE IN YOUR LIFE

WHO	WHAT	WHEN	THE IMPACT	POSITIVE or NEGATIVE OUTCOME

Rather than making notes in this book can I suggest you go to my website <www.budgetblitz.com.au> and download the template.

Once you've completed this table, have a go at the next template*, Major Events in Your Life. Here you need to think about all the major events that have happened in your life and the impact they have had on the way you approach money. Jot down these events in the first column (one per row). For example, you lost your job, got married, got divorced, got sick, got a new job, went on a holiday, and so on. Next to the event, write down when it happened and how much it cost you or how much you earned. Then write down what impact each event had on your overall financial situation at that time, and indicate whether you think that event had a positive or negative effect on your approach to money and your financial status today.

THE MAJOR EVENTS IN YOUR LIFE SO FAR

THE EVENT	WHEN	HOW MUCH	THE IMPACT	POSITIVE or NEGATIVE OUTCOME

Rather than making notes in this book can I suggest you go to my website <www.budgetblitz.com.au> and download the template.

Interesting all of this, isn't it? Can you see a pattern forming?

Now, before you go running off trying to lay blame on any particular person or event in your life for your current money situation, let me now show you how you can process and analyse this information to establish a solid foundation for moving forward.

IT'S ALL ABOUT YOUR MONEY PERSONALITY

Many psychologists will tell you that most of your imprint learning happens when you are very young, and it is from what you see and hear from your parents that determines largely who you are today.

When it comes to money, all of the above (the impact of the key people in your life and the major events you've experienced) combines to form your "money personality".

In other words, your money personality is the answer to why you do what you do with your money. Understand it, control it and change it and you will be in a great position to break out of the pay-to-pay cycle.

When it comes to money personalities you can be one of three types – Spender, Careful, or Savvy. While you certainly have elements of each in your overall make up, one element will be dominant during any period of your life.

Sure, you can change your money personality over time, and that's exactly what many people do. But you don't go from being one personality to another overnight. Just like your overall personality, you don't change into a different one each day (well hopefully not anyway!).

Changing your money personality takes time, and there are a number of elements or traits (in fact, nine) that need to change in order for you to have a different personality. Understanding these traits will shed some light on why you do what you do with your money and, of course, why you are living in the pay-to-pay cycle.

The first and most important of these traits is your **knowledge of money.** Here, the more you know about money and the money world, the more sophisticated your money personality will be and the better you will manage your money.

Unfortunately, far too many people have had a negative experience with money at some stage of their life, either caused by the key people in their life or some kind of major event.

Generally, this leads to negative memories around money being stored in their subconscious. which impacts on their trust with financial institutions and their products. When it then comes to learning more about money, this group of people can go one of two ways.

First, they can become incredibly sceptical about any money education opportunity and never venture out of their comfort zones – unfortunately, leaving them to circulate in the pay-to-pay cycle.

Second, they undertake drastic measures in order to achieve a quick fix. Because they may be under significant financial stress, they can be vulnerable to what I call the "seminar sharks", who charge an arm and a leg to get people hyped up and deluded into thinking they can make millions.

'There are nine elements that need to change in order for you to have a different personality.'

In reality, those attending probably don't have two dollars to rub together; worse still, they are not that money savvy. The outcome can be quite unpleasant, and they may end up signing for financial programs they really can't afford. Their intention to attend a seminar and learn more is admirable, however it is a little misguided due to the fact that they are not that money savvy.

When it comes to seminars or online video series, there are good ones and bad ones. My recommendation is go for the reputable companies and don't pay thousands just to attend. Try and get as much input as you can for free. And whatever you do, don't pay for a workshop on your credit card if you are struggling to repay it. Finally, never forget that just as I don't have a magic wand to fix your money problems overnight, neither do the people who run the seminars.

To make a great free start turn to places like the Australian Government's latest financial literacy initiative <www.moneysmart.gov.au> for quality independent information about money. At the end of the day, quality money knowledge is an absolute must in helping you manage your money better.

Once your money knowledge improves, you'll start to gain greater **confidence** (the second trait) and you'll have a greater chance of making things happen. To me, it's just like cooking. You start off following the recipe line by line. As you gain confidence through increased experience and knowledge, you find yourself rarely referring to the recipe.

'Once your money knowledge improves, you'll start to gain greater confidence.'

Money is the same. The more confident and comfortable you are with money, the more able you will be to make sound money decisions to help you break out of the cycle.

The third trait is your **involvement in money affairs.** Here, the greater your day-to-day active involvement, the greater the chances of you breaking out of the cycle. If you have the knowledge and confidence you will therefore be more predisposed to making things happen or tackling problems head on, rather than sticking your head in the sand and hoping they'll go away.

Being involved with your money affairs enables you to be on the front foot. For example, if you have a problem making your next repayment on a loan, you should be proactive and talk to your lender first to arrange something. I can guarantee you'll be amazed by how responsive they are to proactive people.

Risk (the fourth trait) comes in different forms. Each of us handles it in different ways. While you may be comfortable with taking certain risks with your money, others may not, and that can determine where you are at financially.

For those who understand the different types of risk associated with various financial products and activities (high risk, high return or high risk, no return!), they potentially have a greater chance of managing their money well. If you don't fully understand the different risks and get involved in high risk ventures promising very high returns, you could get caught short. Rather than being fuelled by greed at the prospect of making some real bucks to get out of the pay-to-pay existence, you need to know more. Be careful. Far too many people who had their backs to the wall have been lured into schemes that look like their salvation, only to find it turned out to be the last nail in their financial coffin!

Let me share with you a quick story of a close friend of mine who fell into this sort of hole. He was on an average income with a wife, two kids, a cat, two guinea pigs and a mortgage. He was not too up to speed with all things money, but he really wanted to break free of the pay-to-pay cycle, so he attended a property investment seminar which he thought was going to make things better for him.

'Rather than be fuelled by greed at the prospect of making some real bucks, you need to know more.'

Before he knew it, he and his wife were on a plane to Brisbane to conduct a "free" inspection on a "guaranteed return" investment property. He was so excited that his problems would be over, he signed up on the spot.

Unfortunately, one year down the track the investment not only lost value, it began to make a significant drain on his cash flow. Every month he would have to shell out money for something or other to do with the property. He got to the point where he just couldn't go on taking losses, so he had to sell.

By that stage he owed more than the property was worth, so he had to part with his pride and joy, a 1964 Holden he had painstakingly restored from a wreck. The learning here is that my friend got carried away with the prospect of a great return without investigating and understanding the true level of risk prior to jumping in.

When it comes to the amount of effort you put into your money affairs, the fifth trait, your **work ethic**, can play a key role in breaking out of the pay-to-pay cycle.

Your success largely depends on how disciplined you are. Hence the more energy and focus you put on working out ways to get out of the pay-to-pay cycle, the better off you will be. I mentioned earlier about needing to know how much you really **want** to break out of the cycle – well, this manifests itself in your effort. Therefore, the smarter you work and the more passion you put into it, the greater the chance you'll break out.

The sixth trait, your **spending habits**, looks at a number of factors such as your needs and wants, and your conscious and subconscious behaviour with regard to the purchase of essential and non-essential items. When it comes to essential items that you require to satisfy basic needs (food, clothing, shelter, etc) the way you spend money on them can clearly be influenced by both your conscious and subconscious mind.

For example, if your conscious mind is in control whilst you are shopping from a defined list, you generally end up with what you set out to purchase at a price you pretty much expected.

However, if your subconscious mind takes over whilst you're purchasing the same set of basic needs, you could end up with a higher bill due to the fact that your inner wants start to take over.

Here you will find yourself making impulse purchases or you'll end up buying premium brands and paying more just because you think they are higher quality.

'Essential items spending is clearly influenced by both your conscious and subconscious mind.'

If your conscious mind kicks in when you are buying a luxury item, you may find yourself in a bargaining position or find yourself doing significant research before you make the purchase. Alternatively, if the subconscious mind takes hold you will probably end up paying full price and justifying your purchase by saying that it is a reward for all your hard work.

As you can see, understanding what drives your purchasing behaviour and patterns is critical to managing your money personality, as the more you understand your motivations the better your ability to break out of the pay-to-pay cycle.

The flip side of your spending habits is the seventh trait, your

saving habits. This trait is all about your willingness to accept the concept of sacrificing the "now" for the "future". Sounds pretty hard when you are knee deep in bills with only a limited income! I know. I've been there. And the prospect of someone telling you this seems quite preposterous.

But if you really want to break out of the pay-to-pay cycle you need to get your subconscious mind to focus on wanting something specific.

In other words, focus on a particular goal and commit to it. (I'll show you how to do this in Chapter 2.) From here you need to put your conscious mind into action to make things happen. Instead of following the age-old formula of what's left over after expenses are taken away from income is savings, I suggest a new formula for you to follow.

I call it the **Money Allowable Formula**.

Put as an equation, it looks like this:

I – S – E = MA

That is:
Income *minus* ***Savings*** *minus* ***Expenses*** *equals your* ***Money Allowable****.*

The reason why I have put the savings as a deduction from income is that you must learn how to pay yourself first. This is fundamental to getting into a mindset that operates in the surplus mode and not constantly chasing your tail trying to scrape up enough money to pay for something. A great way to start with savings is with a couple of dollars each pay. Then have your pay officer at work deposit an amount in your savings account. I know this will be tough in the beginning if you're not used to it, but believe me, you'll need the discipline involved here to get you focused on paying yourself first. That's why the savings are subtracted after expenses. (In Chapter 6, I'll share many more savings strategies with you.)

The Money Allowable is essentially your secret weapon to breaking out of the pay-to-pay cycle because, if it is handled properly, it will help you build up cash reserves over and above savings, which you can invest to create an income stream all of its own, thereby giving you additional income to your salary. When you first start using the

Money Allowable Formula, you will definitely find yourself going from a zero Money Allowable status to a positive one, then to a negative one.

Don't despair as this is quite normal, because your money personality will take a little time to adjust to this new approach. Hopefully over time you will get the hang of setting yourself a savings amount and subtracting it out of your income along with expenses. Once you see the ongoing benefits of a surplus, your subconscious mind will take over. Not only will you have found a way to cover your expenses, you will have found a way to save and have money left over to invest.

Speaking of investments, this brings me nicely to the eighth trait, your **attitude to investment**. You may be thinking, how does this affect me getting out of the living from pay-to-pay cycle? A good question – the answer lies in your subconscious.

To explain, let's go back to the example of my friend who bought that investment property. In his case, he leapt into it totally unprepared. Sure, he had good intentions and his attitude to investment was good, but these were more from his conscious mind – he wanted to get a quick fix and to "negative gear".

The problem was, it wasn't a quick fix and he didn't actually understand negative gearing. As you can see, you can have the desire from your subconscious mind, but you need the right knowledge to make the right investment choice. In other words, my friend should have spent more time in his conscious mind learning about the broader range of investment opportunities – how they work, the amount of risk they carry, the appropriate investment balance and the return they will generate. In this way, the consequences of his mistake would have been significantly better.

'You can have the desire, but you need the right knowledge to make the right investment choice.'

The final trait in the discovery process of money personalities is your **tolerance to debt.** The way you view debt can affect the way you handle your finances and, of course, how you can break out of the pay-to-pay cycle. Debt can mean different things to different people, and it is good debt management that basically separates those who can manage to break out the of pay-to-pay cycle, and those who can't. For example, if you see debt as a necessary means to an end to buy a house or a car, you'd probably get a decent deal and pay the loan off diligently over time. You may be a bit sharper and look for the best deals and aim to pay off your debts faster, so it's not so much of a burden on your income. You may, on the other hand, see debt as a great way to leverage your financial position by using a lender's money. Therefore, you strategically use that money to fund an investment and reap the income and tax benefits.

Alternatively, you may see debt in a negative light and try to avoid it as much as you can. Hence, you rarely have any debt or, if you do, you pay it back as fast as you can to get it off your back.

Finally, you may be a person who is quite susceptible to debt and use it pretty regularly as a quick and easy fix to your particular situation. This is probably the worst of all of the perspectives, because here you will generally be faced with multiple debt payments and potentially high interest rates that eat up most of your income. By the way, a comfortable level of debt as a proportion of your income (or income to expense ratio) should be around 20–30 per cent. In other words, only 20–30 per cent of your total income should go to paying back debt.

The greater the debt burden on your income, the harder it is to break out of the pay-to-pay cycle. Hence you need to not only do something about your debt situation, you need to change the way you approach your debt.

WHAT'S IN A MONEY PERSONALITY?

We've had a look at the nine traits that make up your money personality. Now let's have a look at the money personalities themselves in detail. Again, remember the reason why we are delving into these money personalities is once you discover the core traits and link them to core personality, and then link them to the key people and events in your life, you will get a much better picture as to why you are doing what you are doing with your money.

From there, you be able to use the following chapters as a road map to help you break out of the pay-to-pay cycle forever.

As you read each of the short descriptions you'll definitely find yourself saying things like "yep that's like me" or "oh no, I don't do that". Just remember you are made up of parts of each personality, however you are dominant in one personality at the moment. That's why it is natural for you to relate to certain bits of each of the three personalities as you read them.

You will, however, find yourself saying "yes" more often to one of the personalities, and chances are this will be your dominant money personality.

I'll help you discover your own money personality shortly, when I get you to undergo my very own Money Personality Diagnostic!

THE SPENDER MONEY PERSONALITY

For various reasons Spenders find that money goes out faster than it comes in. Many tend to live from pay packet to pay packet and have a limited (or non-existent) method for managing their money. Sometimes they are unable to even pinpoint just where their money goes.

Whether or not they have a good work ethic, their knowledge about how to save and invest is generally low to moderate and they therefore display a lack of confidence in making money-related decisions. Some Spenders mistakenly consider themselves to be savvy due to the way they spend rather than how they invest.

In other words, they use various shopping discount cards just to purchase often un-needed items. They use the discount or money saved as justification for the purchases, which gives them the delusion of being savvy. Many Spenders shy away from seeking money advice because they are afraid of asking what they consider to be dumb questions. Because of this they are unlikely to be aware of the alternative options available.

Spenders tend not to take risks in areas that would most benefit them financially, however they can be lured into not so smart investments due to the promise of a high return. They rarely have investments other than a savings account at a bank.

THE CAREFUL MONEY PERSONALITY

Careful money personalities tend to watch their money quite closely, no matter what level of income they're on. They generally have a system of managing their money, although their system may be a bit rough and ready. They have a moderate level of money knowledge and are open to learning more about money if it comes from a trusted source.

They like to take their time when making financial decisions, because they have a fear of losing their money. They are relatively confident in handling and allocating their money, but they tend to balk at the riskier opportunities, preferring to stick with conservative choices of financial product or investment.

Careful people usually have a strong work ethic and spend the fruits of their labour in a controlled manner although, they do lash out every once in a while (usually very infrequently).

They don't like being in debt, and when borrowing stay in their comfort zone, safe in the knowledge they have the capacity to service the debt.

Most purchases by Careful types are considered and researched.

THE SAVVY MONEY PERSONALITY

Savvy money personalities have a solid level of money knowledge that has been gleaned from constant learning, either from direct education or through trial and error.

A key element of Savvy people is their propensity to listen and learn more about money and the various strategies they can follow to improve their wealth. They are more than willing to accept the input of others and they definitely seek the advice of experts.

Savvy money people generally have a very good work ethic and they expect their money to work equally as hard.

They have a moderate to high level of confidence and appreciate and understand varying levels of risk associated with their money and investments. They like to be involved in their financial affairs but are just as happy to have an expert look after it for them.

Although their spending is controlled, they will not hold back if they really need or want something. They are always on the lookout for good value.

Savvy money personalities are good at managing debt to their advantage, using credit cards and larger loans well, while constantly focusing on reducing their level of non-tax-deductible debt. They are quite analytical although they do have a natural gut instinct they rely on occasionally.

SO WHAT'S YOUR MONEY PERSONALITY? THE MONEY PERSONALITY DIAGNOSTIC

Okay, by now you should have a pretty good grasp of the nine traits and a good overview of each money personality and how they apply to the pay-to-pay world we live in.

I'm sure you even have an inkling of your own money personality, but let's work it out properly.

To reveal your money personality, all you have to do is answer the questions in the following quiz openly and honestly then tally up your responses. The score that with the highest tally indicates your dominant money personality.

One last point before you start. Please answer the questions the way you are at this very minute, not the way you think you should be. By doing this you will get an accurate result. This is an important step in getting in touch with your conscious mind.

Okay, let's go.

1 WHEN YOU'RE SHOPPING FOR GROCERIES DO YOU:

A. Walk up and down the aisles, grab the essentials and also grab a few extra treats
B. Shop regularly using a list and keeping an eye out for products available on special
C. Use your discount and member cards and shop at the places where you get the best prices and value
D. Pop up to the local convenience store and buy what you need

2 WHEN IT COMES TO WORK DO YOU:

A. Spend most of your day thinking about your plans for the weekend
B. Do the best you can
C. Look for ways to improve your career path by diligently going about your job and building a network of contacts
D. Work to live

3 DID YOUR PARENTS TEACH YOU ABOUT MONEY (HOW TO SAVE AND INVEST)?

A. No
B. Sometimes
C. Always
D. Can't remember

4 WHEN YOU GO TO FILL UP THE CAR WITH PETROL DO YOU:

A. Decide to half fill it and end up pumping more petrol than you intended
B. Fill to exactly the amount or level you set out to do
C. Fill up totally at the lowest price you can find and use your credit card for points
D. Fill beyond what you intended and buy a few goodies (chocolates etc) as well

5 WHEN YOU ARE BUYING SOMETHING LIKE A NEW FRIDGE, BED OR TV DO YOU:

A. Take out a "buy now, pay later" deal
B. Pay cash
C. Put it on the credit card and earn points but pay it off just before the interest due date
D. Borrow from a friend or relative to pay for it

6 DO YOU DISCUSS MONEY AND THE INVESTMENT WORLD WITH YOUR FRIENDS?

A. Never
B. Sometimes
C. Often
D. Rarely

7 HOW WOULD YOU FEEL IF YOU HAD A COUPLE OF HUNDRED DOLLARS IN YOUR WALLET?

A. I'd want to spend it.
B. I'd hide it in a secret compartment of my wallet/purse.
C. I'd trust that I would use it for the purpose intended.
D. I'd buy a gift or give some away.

8 HOW OFTEN DO YOU READ THE MONEY AND FINANCE SECTION IN THE MEDIA?

A. Hardly ever
B. Sometimes/usually
C. Religiously
D. Never have

9 DO YOU HAVE A SET OF FINANCIAL GOALS?

A. Sort of
B. I've got them but they are not written down
C. Yes and I refer to them from time to time
D. No

10 HOW WILLING ARE YOU TO ACT ON A HOT SHARE MARKET TIP?

A. Very
B. Never
C. Depends
D. If I'm in the mood

11 YOU PAY YOUR BILLS ...

A. Usually on time but have a tendency to let them slip
B. On time, every time
C. On the very last day before interest kicks in
D. Always late

12 YOU SAVE ...

A. Not much
B. A certain amount each pay
C. Regularly and continually increase the amount saved over time
D. I can't

13 WHERE DO YOU INVEST YOUR MONEY?

A. I don't
B. In a considered high interest savings account
C. In a combination of considered investments
D. It just sits in my normal everyday bank account

14 HOW OFTEN DO YOU READ THE FINE PRINT?

A. Never
B. Mostly
C. All the time
D. Bits of it

15 WHEN IT COMES TO PLANNING YOUR MONEY AFFAIRS FOR YOUR FINANCIAL FUTURE DO YOU:

A. Turn right off and think of something else
B. Diligently set goals and strict budgets
C. Actively seek and rely on professional money and financial advice
D. Hope that it will all take care of itself

16 WHAT WOULD YOU DO IF YOU GOT A $500 BONUS FROM YOUR WORK?

A. Spend it
B. Save it
C. Pay off debt
D. Party

17 HOW OFTEN DO YOU MONITOR YOUR DEBTS?

A. Only when the credit card statement arrives
B. Once a week
C. Once a month
D. Never

18 HOW DO YOU PAY OFF YOUR CREDIT CARD?

A. Mostly the minimum amount
B. Pay it off as soon as you buy something
C. On time every time and pay enough each month to avoid interest charges
D. When I get around to it

19 I SPEND MY MONEY

A. To feel good
B. According to my budget
C. Whenever I need to
D. To survive

20 I ATTEND A MONEY EDUCATION SEMINAR

A. Never
B. Sometimes
C. Frequently
D. Yeah right!

21 BEING IN DEBT MEANS

A. Less to spend
B. A burden that I must pay back as fast as I can
C. Part of life and a way to make money
D. Constant worry

To determine your score simply count all the As, Bs, Cs and Ds you selected, and then add the number of As and Ds together.

Total A + D ________
Total B ________
Total C ________
Total = 21

HOW TO INTERPRET YOUR SCORES

You will most likely have a combination of scores, which means you have elements of each personality. You will, however, have one particular personality that receives a greater score. Even if your scores are within one point of each other, you will still have a definite leaning to that particular personality.

ALMOST EQUAL SCORES

If you scored, say, 8 Bs, 7 Cs and 6 As, it may seem that you are pretty much balanced between each of the three personalities. While there is a definite leaning toward Careful, it would seem that there are still many hangovers from the Spender personality. The goal here should be to reduce the number of Spender elements, that is As and Ds, so that your dominant personality (either B or C in this instance – it can go either way with scores this close) can improve.

DOMINANT AS AND DS

If you scored highest on As and Ds, it means you are heavily dominated by the Spender personality. Even though you may have scored some Bs and Cs, they are not strong enough at present to have an overall effect.

DOMINANT BS

If your highest count was B, this indicates that you are dominated by the Careful personality. Take a look at the other scores you received. If there are more Cs than As and Ds, you have an opportunity to improve and ultimately move to the Savvy personality.

DOMINANT CS

If your highest score was C you are definitely Savvy with your money. If your next highest score was B, I'd expect you to be more conservative in your handling of money (even though you are Savvy). If your second highest score was As and Ds this would indicate that you may be a little more aggressive with your handling of money, as you are not afraid to spend some money to possibly make money.

CHANGING YOUR MONEY PERSONALITY

I mentioned before that changing your money personality is similar to changing your overall make-up and personality. It takes time and motivation, and it certainly doesn't happen overnight.

Sometimes, however, changes are forced upon you. This may happen when you encounter major life events, like death, separation or loss of a job. But for the most part changes to our money personality represent a slow and gradual process.

Let me tell you it is achievable, and anyone with the will to change can do it. Ultimately you should be aiming to have more Savvy scores than the others as this is by far the most advanced money personality. To move from a Spender dominated personality to Savvy a person needs to become more careful with their money. Then they need to acquire a new set of knowledge (that is, understand what financial products and management systems are available). With this knowledge they can look for more efficient ways to spend and ultimately save their money.

Moving from Careful to Savvy requires developing a deeper knowledge of financial products and services and how to use them efficiently.

For example, a Careful person may keep $10,000 sitting in an everyday savings account in a bank, whereas a Savvy money person would definitely have it in a high-interest savings account or working even harder in another investment such as a managed fund or a direct share market investment.

All the Careful person needs to do in this instance is to learn more about the alternative places to invest so they can achieve the same level of security and access but with a much higher return.

"Moving from Careful to Savvy requires developing a deeper knowledge of financial products and services."

Now, being Savvy does not necessarily mean that person knows it all. It just describes the way a Savvy money person uses knowledge to improve their situation. It is definitely a personality that we can all aspire to, but once we reach it the level of knowledge required to stay there increases.

Even though there is more to know, a Savvy money person can keep up to date relatively easily. They probably have a good team of advisors and a positive interest in money, so anything new is not that daunting. Savvy money people realise that having good money skills is a team sport. The better the team the better they will become.

There are, however, lessons a Savvy person can learn from a Spender in terms of being able to enjoy their money and spending it on things that bring them joy. Otherwise, a Savvy person can run the risk of being too tight and not enjoying their life.

"As a big influencer in my life, my mother's Careful money personality rubbed off on me."

One of the biggest barriers to changing a person's money personality is the fear of asking questions.

Some people simply don't ask anything because they are afraid of appearing stupid. Sure, the first time you ask a question you may get tongue-tied, but do it a few times and you will find it comes much more easily. To overcome this, you need to discard the old schoolroom peer pressure feeling and start asking what you want to know.

Another barrier to change is the sheer amount of determination required. As I mentioned above, a big effort is often required to change your money situation. Often it takes longer than initially anticipated and it can be complicated. That's why plenty of focus, energy and discipline is required to make a change. It's just like going on a diet or quitting smoking – you need to make a concerted effort.

SO NOW WHAT?

We've come a long way in this chapter and I hope by now you've got a much better insight into some of the reasons why you do what you do with your money.

My goal is to give you as many tools as I can for you to get beyond the obvious and start thinking about why you are in your current situation. Any supposed "money guru" can go straight for the solution and tell you what to do in "Ten easy to follow steps", but that's not going to get you anywhere and it's certainly not a long-term remedy.

You actually need to understand the core reasons why you do the things you do before you attempt to implement a solution.

That's why I have spent so much time in this chapter getting you in the headspace of understanding the difference between your needs and wants, and getting you to look at your conscious and subconscious money management behaviour.

I also hope I've opened your eyes with regard to the impact key people and major events in your life have had and are still having on your approach to money. Finally, I hope I've helped you discover your money personality and the core traits that drive it.

Before moving on to Chapter 2 I'd like to share with you a quick review of all of the above in real life using someone I know pretty well.

Me.

What you are about to read is a very quick snapshot of my life so far in the context of what we have been talking about in this chapter.

Once you've read this little extract, may I suggest you spend a few moments to reflect on your life. Use the same template as I have to recount your story, and see what answers it provides. Chances are it will reveal what you do with your money!

A PERSONAL INSIGHT

I have always been pretty much in touch with my conscious and subconscious money mind and very much aware of my money personality.

However, there have been times when my money personality has changed due to the major circumstances I've encountered. (By the way, my money personality right now is Savvy, with my scores being C = 17, B = 2 and A & D = 2. Lucky for you, huh? Last thing you want is a guy who writes a book who is a mad spender!).

THE KEY PEOPLE WHO INFLUENCED MY MONEY PERSONALITY:

When it comes to the key people in my life who influenced me in my approach to money, the first is my mother. Being a World War II refugee from Eastern Europe, she is a real worrier about almost everything when it comes to money.

Mum's ultra-conservative by nature, but when it comes to money she is right off the scale. $100 is a huge amount of money to her. She hates being in debt and rarely takes risks. In fact, so afraid is she of not having any money, she always has a spare $50 note tucked away secretly in her purse! Sorry, Mum, I had to tell the world! As one of the big influencers in my life, her careful money personality rubbed off on me.

Subsequently, I have a very "tight" streak when it comes to spending money. (Just ask my brothers at Christmas.)

My second major influencer is my dad. He is an Aussie with an entrepreneurial flair. For pretty much all of his working life he owned and ran his own businesses. From him I learned how to take risks, but also how to save money and manage my cash flow. As a small business owner himself he knew all too well the roller-coaster ride of finances.

Putting little bits away and then investing them was the best thing he ever taught me (this is where I developed the Money Allowable Formula from).

The third key influencer in my life was my boss in my first job at the Australian Stock Exchange.

He was incredible. He not only taught me how to invest, but to also have a positive outlook when it came to money matters.

He was such a positive person that, even on the day of the big share market crash in 1987, he said to me the crash represented a fantastic opportunity for me to make a huge amount of money (not for the short term but in the long term) as it represented a perfect time to buy because the share prices were so low. This man also gave me a sense of confidence with money that I never would have had given my upbringing, a very important trait in a Savvy money personality.

THE MAJOR EVENTS THAT AFFECTED MY APPROACH TO MONEY:

Where do you want me to start? As you've seen in the Introduction, I've had my fair share of significant life events. But I'm sure you have too. The two biggest events to hit me pretty much happened at the same time in 2003, when I was struck down by a mystery illness and my business crashed.

You know how you have bad years? Well, this was mine. Nothing went right for the whole year, from the time the clock chimed 12.00 am on New Year's Eve, 2003, all the way through to early 2004. It was one disaster after another. Why did they happen? Well, the mystery illness is pretty self-explanatory. It remains a mystery to this today. But the business crashing was a culmination of a number of factors, including the loss of key people working in the business and a lack of cash flow. This left the business with massive rents and other outgoings but no-one to create sales.

You don't need long to work out what happened. The impact was devastating, not only on my personal finances but on my overall being. Imagine your pride and joy crumbling right in front of you without being able to do a thing to save it.

In terms of its impact on my personal finances, as I said earlier in this book, I lost almost everything except for some money I had invested over the years (courtesy of the teachings of my dad and my boss from the stock exchange). This experience really shot my confidence to pieces; subsequently, my approach to money for a short time was a negative one. So much so, that for a while I found myself focusing on every cost I had and how I could reduce it, rather than focusing on ways I could make money from multiple sources (that is, create passive income sources).

This was clearly not a good strategy if I was to rebuild and grow my finances.

Looking back I can see it was the influence of my mother's Careful money personality taking over here, and that pretty much put me in a mindset to live life from pay to pay because it was safe. But this was not me. Even so, it was difficult to shake it. The mindset was like a bad habit you know you should stop but you just can't find a way.

My turnaround came in early 2004, and in the strangest possible ways. A friend of mine mentioned he, too, was having major difficulties with his finances and was pretty much resigned to the fact things would not change. In that conversation I suggested various ways he could go to get out of the cycle. Not only was he amazed, but so was I.

At that point it dawned on me that I had the answers, but my confidence was holding me back. Due to my setbacks I was afraid to make the changes necessary to get my money life back on track. I had all the other traits very much down pat, but it was my confidence that was lacking.

"I gave myself permission to focus my energy on making money, rather than trimming costs."

My friend was quite similar, however his overall money knowledge needed topping up, and therefore he had a bit more work to do. Nevertheless, he was now on his way to getting out of the pay-to-pay cycle thanks to a little push from me.

From that point forward it was as if I was transformed back to my old self. It was quite amazing. I could feel the confidence welling up inside and I was brimming with great ideas.

I gave myself permission to focus my energy on making money, rather than spending all my energy on finding ways of trimming costs. The result has been incredible. I made it back on track. In fact, I have made many tracks, and never again will I live from pay to pay or even get close to it.

All thanks to looking inside.

Can you now see, the reason you are in your current financial situation has a lot to do with your money personality? All you must do is to embrace that and put into place the steps I'm about to share with you.

By the end of this book I hope you will be armed with the mindset and know-how to break out of the vicious pay-to-pay cycle.

CHAPTER 2 WORKING OUT WHERE YOU WANT TO BE TOMORROW

I know what you're thinking. Goals. Ugh! Do we have to? Why can't we get to the good bits, where all the answers are laid out on how to get out of the pay-to-pay cycle? Let me remind you that I still don't have a magic wand and no book on earth will give you the answer to every one of your problems.

What I *can* provide, however, is a framework to help you discover things on your own, and then give you some valuable advice about how to make the necessary changes yourself.

In Chapter 1, I took you on a journey to discover why you do what you do with your money. In this chapter I'll get you to do pretty much the same, but with a slight twist. Here, I'll help you discover ways to identify, set, review and celebrate the achievement of your goals across a number of areas in your life – be they personal, professional, financial, health, relationships or fun.

I'll even show you how to enjoy the journey as much as the destination. My goal therefore is to give you the tools to help you set the appropriate strategies in motion, so that you can move toward breaking out of the pay-to-pay cycle and achieve a great financial future. (See, there's a goal right there. Pretty easy, huh?)

Before I start, let's see where you stand when it comes to having goals. Put your hand up (not physically, of course) if you've got some loose goals about where you want to be and what you want to achieve in the future. Now keep it up if you have them written down. Okay. Keep your hand up if you have your goals written down and they have been broken down into different parts of your life such as personal, work and money goals.

If your hand didn't even make it into the air, can you pay special attention to what you are about to read. It will literally change your life.

If your hand made it up for a very short while – good on you for having some sort of direction. But again, I would encourage you to read this chapter very carefully. Not only will it help you cement some of your goals, it will give you the tools to make them happen.

Finally, if your hand was in the air all the way through, I still encourage you to read on. You will find I've got a number of different takes on the traditional ways of setting goals.

When it comes to goals it seems Australians are not that crash hot in setting them. According to a recent study I conducted of 1,125 Australians, only 45 per cent said they had goals. Interestingly, of that 45 per cent, only 25 per cent had them written down and just 5 per cent had them written down and broken up into different areas of their life.

"When it comes to goals it seems Australians are not that crash hot in setting them."

What this tells me is while some people have some idea of what they want out of life, the majority seem pretty much directionless. It's kind of scary when you think about it. Little wonder that many people keep going in circles and living from pay to pay. Without direction how can you see the bigger picture? What you need is a well-defined vision and a well thought out set of goals.

I've experienced life with and without goals, and I can tell you, having a set of goals definitely wins every time. Before that mystery illness of mine I used to have a very well-defined vision and set of goals. I even had a weekly "Things to Do" list written down for my business and personal life that I would diligently follow, crossing each one off as it was achieved.

Plus, I made time to review my list at least once a year. But as soon as I lost my health, I quickly lost focus and direction. Not at any stage during that time did I review my goals or even try to achieve any of them.

The best way I can describe how I felt? Imagine you are on a summer holiday, perhaps by the beach, and the hardest thing you have to do each day is to work out what to eat at lunch or dinner. You develop an "it's all too hard" kind of feeling. That's how I felt.

It was really weird not having any direction, especially as I had always been the kind of person who had goals and "To Do" lists. If you've been in a similar situation, you'll probably relate to this. That feeling of nothingness can really take hold.

On the other hand, if you are lucky enough not to have had any setbacks, remember one thing: no matter what happens to you, stay focused on your goals.

Of course, be prepared to make changes as the situation dictates, but never, I repeat, never lose sight of your goals or, worse still, let yourself get into the situation where you don't have any. If you let this happen, you'll experience exactly what happened to me. You'll lose direction and confidence, and your whole world will feel like it is closing in on you.

Trust me, I've been there. It's so easy to fall into a day-to-day existence when your confidence is low, and unchecked this will definitely affect your money management ability and drop you smack bang in the middle of the living from pay-to-pay cycle.

Now if you are reading this and thinking "Uh-oh, I don't have any goals", don't fret.

The next section is just what the doctor ordered!

CHAPTER 2

YOU NEED A CLEAR VISION TO GET OUT OF THE CYCLE

To get things back on track you need to focus on your vision of the future. This will help you concentrate on the things in life that matter to you. From here you can put together your sets of goals.

I'll come back to goals shortly. First, let me help you explore what your vision of your future looks like. Now, before you say "Hey isn't this book all about finding out how to stop living from pay to pay?" Think about a person without a vision. How are they going to get somewhere without one? Sure they can simply bounce along through life, but in general these people end up with pretty shaky financial lives and struggle from pay to pay. Hence they will always end up in a situation where money controls them rather them controlling their money. Therefore, if you have a clear vision of who and what you want to be, you'll definitely stand a greater chance of breaking out of the pay-to-pay cycle than a person who has no vision.

It's all about knowing where you are going. Just like, for example, when you're going on a Sunday drive. Nine times out of ten you don't just hop in the car and drive. Your vision of a successful Sunday is to spend a nice day with your significant other or your family. From this vision comes a set of goals which pretty much determine where you go and what you do.

If, however, you take off out of the garage without any idea of why or where you're going your perfect day may not turn out as you hoped. Even though at the start this may be quite exciting as the anticipation of the unexpected and unknown kicks in, it can quickly sour as the kilometres and time whiz by without a defined ending in sight.

If your experience is anything like I've encountered over the years, a little skirmish may break out between you and your significant other. Then it all starts to go downhill pretty fast and the perfect day turns into the perfect storm.

Without a clear vision and goal you didn't discover anything new or experience anything different. Unfortunately, all that happened was your little drive ended up costing you money for petrol and some emotional energy! The same goes for your money life. If you've got no vision and no goals you could very well end up spending time and money doing the same thing over and over and always going back to what you know. You'll be stuck in the same old cycle.

To get out of this cycle you need to develop a clear vision of what you want to achieve out of life. Yes, out of life! I know life's impossible to predict, but you have to have some kind of vision so you have something to really aim for.

Once you've got your vision set, you can then put together your goals, which all ultimately add together to achieve your vision.

So how does this work? Simple. To create a vision you need to go into fast forward mode and think about your life many years in the future: what you achieved and what others are saying about you. Sounds spooky but let me explain.

"If you've got no vision and no goals, you'll be doing the same thing over and over with money.

The best way to think about this is to imagine what someone would say about you on the day of your retirement from the workforce or on your seventy-fifth birthday. The answers lie in the following questions:

1. What three things do you need to do every day to keep motivated on a personal level and on a work level?

2. What are your five most important personal values? (For example: ambition, individuality, equality, integrity, service, responsibility, accuracy, respect, dedication, diversity, improvement, fun, loyalty, credibility, honesty, innovativeness, teamwork, excellence, accountability, empowerment, quality, efficiency, empathy, accomplishment, courage, wisdom, independence, security, compassion, friendliness, discipline, generosity, persistency, optimism, dependability, flexibility.)

3. Instead of working, what would you do?

4. Looking back, what will you not regret?

5. How have you made a difference in your career, personal life and spiritual life?

6. How have you made a difference?

I know these questions are pretty confronting, but believe me, you need to go through this soul-searching exercise to get a grip on who you are and what you want to achieve. After, you can set your goals and adjust your money life. I'll give you a chance to answer these questions in a moment. But remember, when you are doing so, take your time and answer each one as a sentence or short paragraph.

Once you've done this you can start to write your own personal vision statement. All you need to do is bring together each of the answers into one big statement about yourself. It can be as long as you like, but since you are writing it from the point of view of when you are seventy-five, you need to write it as if you've actually achieved everything already.

This will give you a blueprint you can build your goals around. One last point: you need to write your vision in the first person as this will give you true ownership.

No doubt things will always change in your life, therefore I recommend you review your vision statement at the end of every year. You may be surprised to find that, despite the changes in your day-to-day life, your full vision statement may go unchanged for some time. This is a good thing; it will give you stability in your path forward.

Now, to give you a hand in putting your vision together, here's a quick snapshot of what mine looks like:

"On the day of my retirement I was remembered as:

A happy, approachable and inspirational character who had a great passion and dedication to the improvement of financial knowledge across Australia and around the world through my public presentations, webinars, books, articles and TV appearances. I was a successful entrepreneur who valued honesty and integrity and encouraged excellence in all my work colleagues. I had a fun and happy demeanour and used humour as my communication tool. I was a warm caring family person who was never afraid to get out of my comfort zone when it came to adventure, personal and financial matters. I was financially secure and healthy most of my life and a loving partner, father and community-focused man who was generous with my time, knowledge and money."

As you can see, nowhere in the above do I say I want a big house with a pool, a good job, millions of dollars, heaps of assets, a great healthy family, a close set of friends or a flash car. The vision is what I want to aspire to; the goals are what I put in place to get there. Remember in Chapter 1 when I covered at length the difference between your subconscious and conscious mind? Well it comes into play again when you're setting your vision. In other words, if you really aspire to getting out of the pay-to-pay cycle and want to have a better life, you must first start in your subconscious and make a commitment to do something. Create your vision, get it on paper and make it happen.

Now it's your turn

Time to put your vision statement together! Hop on to my website <www.budgetblitz.com.au> to download this template or just use a separate piece of paper:

1. What three things do you need to do every day to keep motivated on a personal level and on a work level?

1. ______________________________

____

2. ______________________________

____

3. ______________________________

____

2. What are your five most important personal values? (For example: ambition, individuality, equality, integrity, service, responsibility, accuracy, respect, dedication, diversity, improvement, fun, loyalty, credibility, honesty, innovativeness, teamwork, excellence, accountability, empowerment, quality, efficiency, empathy, accomplishment, courage, wisdom, independence, security, compassion, friendliness, discipline, generosity, persistency, optimism, dependability, flexibility.)

1. ______________________________
2. ______________________________
3. ______________________________
4. ______________________________
5. ______________________________

3. Instead of working what would you do?

4. Looking back at your life what will you not regret?

5. How have you made a difference in your career, personal life and spiritual life?

6. How have you made a difference?

____
____
____
____

Now once you have the words or sentences, put them into paragraph form like I did with mine.

Hint: Begin your vision statement with "*When I retire, I would like to be remembered as…*" as this will immediately put you in the past tense.

____
____
____
____
____
____

This will most likely take you a good hour to put together properly. Once you've got it, leave it overnight and come back to it. I can guarantee fresh ideas will come to you. This is a time-hungry exercise but put it into perspective. Here you are talking about your life, and a few hours setting a vision in order to set goals and set your financial world straight, is time worth spending.

SETTING GOALS

Mark Twain once said "The secret of getting ahead is getting started. The secret of getting started is breaking your complex overwhelming tasks into small manageable tasks, and then starting on the first one".

I love this quote for two reasons. The first, it pretty much sums up the art of successful goal setting, and secondly, it describes exactly the process you are experiencing in this chapter.

You've now got your vision statement, so the next step is to identify and set a series of short-term and long-term goals to ultimately achieve the vision, plus learn techniques to make that happen.

When it comes to goals, I tend to group them into seven categories:

1. Financial How much do you want to earn? What value of assets do you want? How quickly do you want to pay off your debts?
2. Career What sort of job do you want? What level do you want to achieve? Do you want to run your own business? Do you want to set up a passive income stream business?
3. Relationships Do you want a partner? A family?
4. Health Do you what to change your fitness? Your diet? Your weight?
5. Education Do you want to achieve a certain level of knowledge or accreditation? If you have kids, what about their education?
6. Charity Do you want to contribute to the community? If so, how?
7. Fun How do you want to enjoy yourself? Travel? Parties? Local events?

There are two underlying factors with each of the above categories. The first is your overall attitude to life. Again, your subconscious mind plays a very big part in this, and given that it drives your wants, it's in your best interest (if you want to achieve your goals and hence your overall vision) to keep a positive attitude. Being positive breeds confidence, confidence breeds involvement and involvement breeds results.

The second factor is money, and it has a huge impact on how you set and achieve your objectives. Why? Simple, a great proportion of your goals, whether they be financially based or otherwise, will involve money in some way. For example, money will obviously fit into your financial goals, it will fit into your career goals by determining how much you want to earn and it will fit into your relationship goals by determining whether you want to get married or have a child. It will even fit into when you want to have fun, because a holiday will certainly cost money. In all instances, money plays a part.

Therefore, when you are setting your goals, always be aware that money will sooner or later have an impact. So best to try and plan for its impact when you start setting your goals.

When you are in the pay-to-pay cycle, setting goals with a positive attitude can be a trifle difficult as your frame of mind may not be that positive, and the money you have flowing in may not be able to go toward achieving some of your goals.

The trick here is to set small, highly achievable but short-term goals as well as setting larger more challenging long-term goals. The short-term goals will give you the confidence to keep on going with sufficient confidence to tackle the bigger long-term goals.

PUTTING YOUR GOALS INTO ACTION

Now you know the different types of goal categories and the factors that influence them, it's time to start putting them into some form of logical sequence.

The easiest way to do this is to use my Your Goals template, and split your goals into six months, one year, five years, ten years, twenty years, thirty years, forty years and fifty years. Then use each category as a base. You will need to make each goal make sense by applying my WAMIT Formula for setting goals:

W **Written**
Write them down. If it's not written it's not a goal!

A **Achievable**
Can you **achieve** them? Are they realistic?

M **Measurable**
Can you **measure** the results by dollars or a percentage?

I **Inspirational**
Do they **inspire** you? Are they big enough?

T **Timed**
Set a **time** and **date** limit.

Give it a go using the template that follows. Again, take your time completing it, as this can potentially change the course of your future, especially if you are presently in what seems to be a never-ending cycle.

Hint: When you are completing the template, visualise your goal and do as I do: assume you have already achieved it then write it down in the corresponding time period following the WAMIT Formula.

Be specific. So instead of writing "I want to own a house" in the five-year financial cell, write something like "I want to own a four-bedroom, three-bathroom, three-car garage home with entertainment room, a great view of the sea on a very big block of land close to the city".

Put a time and date stamp on it ("I want it by November 20XX") and you've got it. Then, to get your subconscious mind to focus on achieving that goal, close your eyes and visualise it in even more detail ("the house will be cement rendered, painted white with a huge entertaining deck at the back, which leads off a large kitchen area with floor to ceiling windows that capture sunlight and look out on the breathtaking view").

By doing this, you will not only motivate yourself, you'll get your subconscious into achievement overdrive. If however you do experience a problem filling out the cells for the thirty-, forty- and fifty-year time horizons, just refer to your vision statement and work back from there.

When you have several goals in each cell, you'll need to give each one a priority. The best way to do this is use a simple number system, where 1 is the highest priority going down to 5, the lowest priority. I recommend that you don't have more than five goals per cell, as it will start to become overwhelming, and you will end up losing attention for the most important ones. If that happens you will find yourself in the old cycle all over again.

Finally, don't set your goals too low; if the goal is too easy, you could lose faith in goal setting and stop writing down your goals – the most important part of the process.

All you need to do is try and set your goals so that they are slightly out of your immediate reach. No doubt it will challenge you, but there's nothing sweeter than achieving something you had to work really hard for!

Hint: If you are in a relationship, complete the template individually first, then come together and compare, discuss and combine.

How interesting is that going to be? Don't be afraid to have individual goals interleaved in your combined goals template. You need to have individual as well as joint pursuits as long as it is all positive for the relationship.

Be prepared for diversity, but if you see problems early, perhaps it may be an opportune time to see someone impartial like a relationship counsellor.

YOUR GOALS TEMPLATE

(Hop on to <www.budgetblitz.com.au> to download this template)

Today's Date:								
Your Goals	6 months	1 year	5 years	10 years	20 years	30 years	40 years	50 years
Financial								
Career								
Relationships								
Health								
Education								
Charity								
Fun								

MAKING YOUR GOALS COME ALIVE

We've covered a lot already with vision statements and setting goals, and hopefully you've got a better idea of putting together a set of goals to give you a path forward.

Now comes the fun part of making your goals come alive. Having them written down is one thing, but then you need to put them into action and get a result – and that's completely different.

Remember the Mark Twain quote? To achieve your goals you need to break them down into smaller chunks. That's why you need a "Things to Do List" to get things done, otherwise you have a big list of broad items that will never get attended to. This is especially true when it comes to financial matters and goals. Many people leave them to last as they are afraid of them, they're simply not interested or they don't know what to do. The result is they do nothing.

To get out of the pay-to-pay cycle you definitely need a disciplined approach to putting things in an action plan format so you can tick them off one by one. Despite the fact the gains may not seem that large each time, you need to hang in there – all the little wins add up to the achievement of the bigger goal.

When it comes to my expertise in putting "Things to Do" lists together, my early knowledge came from my dear old mum who opened my eyes to these simple but very powerful goal management and delivery tools.

Mum had a list for the whole family, featuring dates and action items for things ranging from holidays to school fetes, and even building times when we had improvements done around our home. Each week she would type out the list (on a manual typewriter, I might add), and on it she'd put the things she or Dad had to do (like pay the electricity bill, book accommodation for the holiday, do the banking, etc) and then she'd attach it to the fridge door for all the family to see.

As each action item was completed she would ever so diligently put a line through it, then put a great big tick at the end. I think she really enjoyed the ticking off part as I can still remember her hand fly off the page right up into the air! Our house at times seemed like a military installation but, by crikey, was my mum incredibly organised. Seriously, though, a "Things to Do List" can save you hours and give you and your partner or family some real direction.

The format of a "Things to Do List" is totally up to you. You really need to be comfortable with it otherwise you won't end up using it. To give you a hand, however, I've included below the Things to Do List template I've developed and have been using for many years. (Again, it is also available to download from <www.budgetblitz.com.au>.)

As you can see, it starts out by giving you the choice of creating a monthly or weekly list.

Personally, I prefer a monthly "Things to Do List" as it gives me sufficient time to achieve my action items. If I had a weekly list I suspect I would have to carry many of the items forward from week to week. When you do this you ultimately defeat the purpose of the whole list. You should be crossing things off the list not transferring ones you couldn't complete!

The aim of the "Things to Do List" is therefore to identify the actual items you need to do to achieve your goal. So, if one of your goals is to save up a certain amount of money to become an emergency reserve of cash to smooth out fluctuations in your cash flow, then one of your action items (you can have more than one action item per goal) could be to set up a high interest savings account. Another action item could be to ask your pay officer at work to automatically deduct a certain amount each pay into this account, and so on. You see what I mean? These action items are simply a list of things you need to do to get things done.

Speaking of which, as you can see in the template I put in the date completed and tick the item off as I write in the date. Yikes! I've become my mother!

THINGS TO DO LIST – PRIORITY FORMAT

FOR MONTH BEGINNING: (INSERT DATE) OR FOR WEEK BEGINNING: (INSERT DATE) OR FOR TODAY: (INSERT DATE)					
Priority	Goal	Goal Category	Action Item (or thing you have to do)	Date Completed	Ticked Off
1					
2					
3					
4					

A DAILY DOSE

Whilst the "Things to Do List" is definitely your passport to achieving your goals, you also need to do a few other key things to ensure you actually achieve them.

The first is to put your goals in a prominent place and read them out loud every day. I read mine each morning just before I start work. Doing this reminds me of what I am aiming for, and it helps me focus on what I have to do.

I keep my goals in two places. The first is on my computer and the second on my fridge door. I know it's a bit of a hangover from my mum's idea, but to me, seeing my goals on the fridge door every morning (and every time I go to the fridge) really keeps me focused.

I keep them there all the time, even when my friends or relatives come around. Why hide them? I am totally proud of what I am aiming for. They should (and do) respect me for that.

You're probably thinking that's a bit risky, as sometimes family and friends can be a tad negative with these sort of things. But it needs to be seen by you and your immediate partner or family. You're the ones who matter.

The second is to get support from a person very close to you (either your partner or closest positive-minded relative). Here you need to tell them what you are doing and ask them if they can be a shoulder to cry on if things don't go exactly as you plan.

If you don't have any relatives, may I suggest you look to a life coach, who will be able to provide you with all the support and encouragement you need.

CELEBRATE YOUR LITTLE WINS AS THEY BECOME BIG WINS

A word of warning when it comes to goals and setting out to achieve them! That is, try not to get too engrossed by them. By that I mean don't become too obsessive about achieving them, like cutting back on all areas of your life just to achieve your goals. Goals need to be free flowing. Being too hard on yourself will end up in you giving up.

Things take time to change and, as I said in Chapter 1, you can't change your money personality and habits overnight. It is the same with re-aligning your goals and getting out of the pay-to-pay cycle.

Your best bet is to enjoy the journey rather than getting caught up in the hot pursuit of a goal. By all means go for your goal, but don't put your life on hold just to achieve it. Getting out the pay-to-pay cycle will take time, so just enjoy the ride along the way. I know your journey may not be all beer and skittles, but if you take the attitude that things are always improving, you will not only enjoy the little moments when they come, you'll really enjoy the big achievements.

One thing I always do when I achieve a goal or when I complete a "Things to Do" action item, is celebrate. Now, before you go out and party like crazy, let me qualify this by saying, the size of the goal and the degree of difficulty I have to endure in order to achieve it are in direct relation to the level of celebratory activities I undertake.

"Definitely take the time to savour your success ... it will inspire you to get on with your next one."

In other words, if it's simply achieving a "Things to Do" action item, I generally put a line through that item, put a date completed on it and tick it off – just like Mum did!

When I achieve a major goal, however, that has been tough to achieve, I reward myself by buying something for the home that I will enjoy. Definitely take the time to savour your success, and it will inspire you to get on with the next one pronto!

HARNESS YOUR OWN ENERGY

I hope by now you totally get that in order for you to break out of the pay-to-pay cycle you need to have a clear vision of where you want to go, a well thought out set of goals and a detailed "Things to Do List" of action items.

All of this is great. However, you really need to have the proper drive to actually do something.

This energy can come from inside yourself, from your partner or from a close friend. But at the end of the day the buck stops with you. You are the one who has to get up in the morning and look at your goals. Plus, you are the one who goes to bed at night knowing whether you have or haven't achieved your goals.

The choice is yours.

You need to take control because you should aim to be in control of your money and not let money control you. Again, there's no fairy godmother nor is there a magic wand I can wave to help you achieve all of your goals easily. You need to go it alone, otherwise you'll never learn what to do. If your family is close and supportive, I suggest you harness their energy and get them to see what you are setting out to achieve.

Who knows, what you are doing might rub off on them!

It's quite amazing how even the smallest amount of encouragement can go a very long way, helping you to achieve your goals much, much faster.

If, on the other hand, those around you begin to question your goals and whether or not you'll be able to achieve them, quickly look outside your immediate social sphere and find other people or things that inspire you to achieve your goals. I know it sounds corny, but I like to take myself off to see an uplifting movie to inspire me.

Do whatever works for you, but never forget negative thinking will only lead to failure. The last thing you need is someone giving you negative thoughts when you are in a tough spot and trying to break out of the pay-to-pay cycle.

The bottom line is that a key ingredient to getting out of this cycle is to have what I've been talking about in this chapter: a good vision, solid goals, a trusty pen to tick off your action items and plenty of self-focus, energy and discipline to make it happen.

CHAPTER 3
KNOWING THE DIFFERENCE BETWEEN WHAT YOU EARN AND WHAT YOU SPEND!

Having a good handle on where your money goes is a fundamental ingredient in breaking out of the pay-to-pay cycle.

If you've got no idea of where your money is going (regardless of how much you earn) you're actually flying blind, so the chances of you breaking out are pretty limited. What you really need to do is find a method of managing your money flows that suits your day-to-day lifestyle, so you can discover where every cent is coming from and where it's going.

Speaking of methods, in this chapter I'm going to share with you a few of my tried and tested techniques for tracking your money flows, plus I'll share a few other tricks, like finding out what your net profit or loss is per year. Sounds like fun, huh?

I've also got plenty of templates and Excel spreadsheets to help you with your day-to-day money management. Now you can have all the templates in the world, but without commitment you'll get nowhere. That's why I really need you to promise me you'll do the homework I talk about in this chapter. By making a concerted effort to do this, it will not only set the scene for the rest of the book, it will get you on the path to breaking out of the pay-to-pay cycle. When it comes to knowing the difference between what you earn and what you spend, you need to get accurate figures on all forms of income you earn and all forms of expenses you pay out.

Sounds pretty simple, but in reality, these figures can be tough little cookies to work. When it comes to money, far too many of us really have no idea where it all goes. Are you one of them? Think hard before you answer that question, as I have some research that may blow your mind when it comes to tracking money coming in and money going out.

Recently I conducted a survey where I asked, "Do you have any idea where your money is going?" This is what I found: 48 per cent of people had some sort of an idea in their head but it was definitely not written down, 15 per cent knew exactly where it was going down to the cent and 37 per cent admitted that they had absolutely no idea at all (apart from the big things like rent or the mortgage).

"Budgeting is like a public transport ride to work – mind-numbing but absolutely necessary."

Read that again: 37 per cent had absolutely no idea. Hmm. Which one are you again?

My good mate Dave is a great example here of someone who knows exactly where their money is going. I've known him for pretty much all my life, and he has always been the same with his money. He's going to hate me for saying this, but he's your normal everyday bloke who, despite earning a normal income always somehow manages to achieve a monthly surplus of $500. Now, that's after all his expenses for himself and his wife (and their dog!). To make all this happen, Dave uses an annual budget he created himself on an Excel spreadsheet. He tracks all his money coming in (salary, money from his two investment properties, tax refunds, etc) and expenses over a twelve-month period. Ironically, he says he hates budgets, but he nevertheless does them and reviews them every few months. In fact, there's never a day that goes by when Dave is not watching every dollar he spends physically and remotely (automatic payments, debt payments, etc).

Dave's system is remarkably similar to what most businesses follow whereby they set an annual budget, break it down into monthly allocations and then monitor it as often as possible. Dave grew up on a commercial farm where his father had to manage the entire property, including the finances, so you can see where he gets this business-like attitude from.

In the thirty-odd years I've known him, Dave's system has never let him down and he's never once slipped into the pay-to-pay cycle as a result.

To me, he's a shining example of cash flow management. He may not be the world's richest man, or the savviest investor, but he's always got cash in his wallet and is always enjoying himself.

One thing Dave says about budgets rings very true: they are downright boring to do. But he sees it like a train ride to work: "It may take a lot of time out of your life and be a bit mind-numbingly boring, but it's absolutely necessary for you to get the things you want."

IT'S EASIER TO BUDGET WHEN YOU'VE ACTUALLY GOT MONEY TO BUDGET WITH

I'm not too sure where this heading came from, but I think it's probably a quote from my dad, who always used to tell me that you needed real numbers in order to put together a real budget. Putting together estimates will only get you so far. A budget must be based on something concrete. That's why he taught me from an early age to be very aware of every cent I spent. I'd write down in my little pocket book what I bought, the time I bought it (don't know why I did that but it seemed quite official at that stage), the date and how much it cost. I know this was weird for a schoolboy, and luckily my school mates didn't know what I was doing as they probably would have ribbed me to such a point I stopped doing it altogether. Who knows, my life could have turned out totally differently.

This exercise of writing down everything I bought and how much I spent really opened up my eyes. It showed me that my pocket money was quite vulnerable to the pleasures of the school canteen and multiple cream buns and pies!

But enough about my childhood. What about you? Can you honestly say that you know exactly where you spend your money? If you can, congratulations and well done for achieving what thousands of Australians are striving for. You can go to the top of the class for the moment, and while you are there, have a quick read of this section just as a refresher. (Hopefully, you will even pick up a few new techniques.)

If you are really pushed to know where your money is going, then please read the next bit very carefully, as you are about to discover a simple but very effective set of ideas and templates that will be a real eye-opener for you. Best of all, if you use them the way I suggest and put some in some real effort (and yes, you will have to put in a fair bit), you'll stand a great chance of busting right out of the pay-to-pay cycle!

GETTING THE RIGHT INFORMATION

Let me kick off with what I call the data collection phase. Here, I'm going to ask you to start out on a journey that will take you about four weeks. Yes, four weeks! I know this might seem like a long time but, hey, never forget it's probably taken you much longer to get into your pay-to-pay cycle, so in the scheme of things it's really nothing.

Think of it as your first investment.

Not in money, but in you.

None of this money stuff happens overnight. You've got to give it a real go and, let's face it, it's only four weeks of your life. Why four weeks, you ask? Well, that's pretty much the minimum amount of time it can take for you to collect the hard data on your spending patterns.

To start you off, here's a simple Money Tracker template that I've developed over the years, which you can use to gather the data.

Download it from <www.budgetblitz.com.au>, print it out and keep a copy with you at all times. Fold it into your wallet, purse, handbag, computer bag or whatever. Just take it everywhere you go. I know it sounds very old school and non-digital in a world of spending tracker apps from your bank, but trust me, it's a brilliant, fail-safe system.

MONEY TRACKER TEMPLATE

Week:				
Week Beginning:				
Date	What did I spend my money on?	Category (*see list below)	$	Did I Really Need It? (Y/N)

* Category – You must choose one of these for each item you spend money on – Housing (rent, mortgage), Home Maintenance, Utilities and Telecommunications, Insurance, Transport, Food, Clothes, Education, Health/Medical, Personal (alcohol, cigarettes, etc) Hobbies/Sport, Holidays, Gifts, Pets, Repayments.

Filling in this template is going to require a fair bit of concentration and, indeed, discipline on your behalf. I'm going to tell you bluntly that it is a real bugger to fill out, as you are going to have to remind yourself to fill it out every time you spend a cent. On the positive side, the results will be amazing; this little exercise will help you discover (perhaps for the first time in your life) where your money is actually going ... right down to the nearest cent.

To ensure you fill in your Money Tracker every time, try hard to follow these steps. I know it's going to be a bit tough, especially if you've never done anything like this before, but take it easy and you'll be surprised how it will quickly become second nature.

First up, write in the "Week" column (in the top left-hand corner) the week you are working on (Week 1 of 4, Week 2 of 4, etc). Then insert in the "Week Beginning" column the date you are starting from for that week. As a suggestion do it on a Monday to Sunday basis. In the "Date" column write the date you made the purchase, then in the "What did I spend my money on?", column write in what you spent your money on. When you are filling it in be sure to include everything (and I mean everything).

By that, I mean things like your morning coffee, newspapers, your favourite magazine, tolls, fares, lunches, grocery bills, rent, rates, debt repayments, etc. In fact, no matter how small the amount, you absolutely need to capture it. Otherwise you are just wasting your time with this whole exercise. If you have a number of electronic payments that come out during that week, you'll need to include these into the "What did I spend my money on?" column as well. The best way to find out these amounts is to grab bank statements for your savings accounts, personal loans, home loans, buy now, pay later statements, car leases and credit cards.

"No matter how small the amount, you absolutely you need to capture it or you are wasting your time."

Your statements are a great place to find what you've been spending. They are especially useful in helping you pick up those little ATM withdrawals and tap-and-go transactions. Annual payments, such as insurance or car registrations, that might fall outside these four weeks, must still be included. But put them as the last items your Week 4 Money Tracker template. (Just put the word "annual" after the description in the "What did I spend my money on?" column.) Because you need to capture everything you do with your money, you need to collect this data here. But you will treat it slightly different when you tally up all the figures.

In the "Category" column, choose from any of the categories listed under the template. Remember, you must include one only for each item. This will come in handy in the next phase when we analyse your spending. In the "$" column put in how much you spent. Please put in the actual amount – even down to the cent! (Yes, down to the cent.). And, finally, in the "Did you really need it?" column put in a Yes or a No. In other words, answer the question of whether you really needed what you bought. Don't analyse this when you do it. We'll come back to that later.

Okay, I fully appreciate that there's a fair bit to do. But trust me, once you start (and the hardest thing to do is to start), it will become second nature. You may even find yourself continuing to do this well after the four weeks are finished. Or maybe not!

MAKING SENSE OF YOUR MONEY TRACKER TEMPLATE

After four weeks of filling out your Money Tracker template you should have a fair amount of data that you can start analysing. If your records were anything like mine when I first did this, I can completely sympathise. Well, help is now at hand. I have developed a few more templates that will help make some real sense of all this data.

CATEGORISING YOUR SPENDING

First things first. We need to put some structure around your spending by creating some categories. By using the template below, all you have to do is to total each of the categories put down for the purchases you made during the four-week period. (Please note, that if you paid a lump sum for any of your annual expenditures, such as insurance, during the four-week period, you'll need to divide it by twelve and only use the monthly amount in the template).

Rather than making this a manual process, hop onto my website <www.budgetblitz.com.au> and download this template. It is a spreadsheet with in-built calculations. You can enter amounts for each category and it automatically adds it all up for you.

You'll also notice in the template there are headings called "Fixed" and "Variable". These will help show you that things like your housing costs are fixed costs which can't be changed that easily, while things like housing maintenance are things where you generally have some control over the spending. Many people would argue that food, utilities and transport costs are fixed costs; I'd argue that they are variable, as I believe (and you don't have to agree) you can always shop smarter for your food, be more energy efficient with your usage of electricity and gas (hence saving on your utilities bills), be more phone savvy by getting better deals for your phones and reduce your transport costs (albeit slightly in some cases) by driving less, carpooling, etc. All this talk about fixed and variable will make sense in a few minutes time.

YOUR CATEGORY EXPENSES TEMPLATE

Category Expenses	$ per month
Fixed	
Housing (eg rent, mortgage)	
Insurance	
Health/Medical	
Total Fixed	
Variable	
Home Maintenance	
Utilities and telecommunications	
Transport	
Food	
Clothes	
Education	
Personal (alcohol, cigarettes, etc)	
Hobbies/Sport	
Holidays	
Gifts	
Pets	
Repayments (personal loans, credit cards)	
Total Variable	
TOTAL EXPENSES	

ARE YOU IN THE BLACK OR IN THE RED?

Once you've established your total monthly expenses (from your Category Expenses template) you now need to get your total income for that same period.

By total income I mean your after-tax wage, any after tax interest or dividends you received, or any other allowances (such as Centrelink) that come into your bank account. You can get most of this information from your pay slips or from your bank statements.

Hint: To work out a monthly figure from a fortnightly wage simply multiply the fortnightly figure by 26 and then divide by 12. If you are receiving weekly payments, multiply by 52 and then divide by 12 to give you the monthly figure. As far as templates go, this one's pretty straightforward. (Again, you can download it from my website to make things easier.)

YOUR PROFIT AND LOSS TEMPLATE

Your Total Income and Expenses	$ per month
Your after-tax wages	
Your partner's after-tax wages	
Other income (second job, etc)	
Interest Received	
Dividends	
Centrelink Payments	
Your Total Income	
minus	
Total Expenses (from your Category Expenses template)	
Net surplus or deficit	

Okay. Now comes the sixty-four million dollar question. Are you in a surplus or deficit position? Or to use the company terminology, are you showing a profit or a loss?

Clearly the goal is for you to show a surplus. That's exactly what you should be aiming for. However, if you are in the pay-to-pay cycle you will probably be in a deficit ... or at very best breakeven. If, however, you have completed each of these templates and are showing a surplus and you know very well you are not there at all, go back and recheck your calculations as you may not have included a few expenses. (Hint: the expenses that occur over the twelve months, which you must divide up and still include, could be missing.)

Even if you are still showing a surplus after a recalculation you may still not be in any position to break out of the pay-to-pay cycle if you are barely covering expenses and not building a reserve for the future. By reserve, I mean a pool of savings that you can draw upon in times of need to tide you over between difficult months. The way to build this reserve is not to try and save what's left over because, let's face it, that's not going to happen if you are in the pay-to-pay cycle and totally focused on paying expenses. You have to do it before you set aside money for your expenses.

Remember the Money Allowable Formula (I – S – E = Money Allowable, where I = Income, S = Savings and E = Expenses), which I introduced in Chapter 1? Here you need to focus on the concept of paying yourself first (no matter how much you start off with) and then pay off your expenses.

"Enjoy your life, but if you want to get out of the cycle, cut back on unnecessary things."

This is a tough ask in the beginning, but a very necessary one, as it will motivate you to start thinking about smarter ways of spending your money. In other words, those Variable Expenses I mentioned in the Category Expenses template can now be looked at in a different light. First and foremost, you need to ask yourself the question, do I really need that item? The answer is relatively clear if you go back to your Money Tracker template and look for every item where you answered "No" in the "Did I really need that?" column. Now, by simply identifying all of these "Nos" you'll be able to make relatively quick work of reducing your expenditure on those things that are not absolutely necessary.

Let's face it, you were the one who said those items were unnecessary when you were filling in your Money Tracker, therefore it should be very easy for you to not buy them again. Right?

Come on. I know you are not nodding your head that confidently here. Look, you've got to enjoy your life, but if you are in the pay-to-pay cycle and want to get out of it, you can at least cut back on perhaps half of those so-called unnecessary items. Can't you?

To make this really come alive, let's turn them into dollars just for some fun. Go back now and add up how much you have spent on the so-called unnecessary items during the four-week period and you'll see what I mean. What if you cut that figure by fifty per cent? How much extra cash would you have to play with?

All you need to do with this money is to start re-allocating it. Some for savings and some for other necessary expenses. Trust me; you can do it. Again, it's going to take some commitment from you, but you must stick with it if you are going to get out of the pay-to-pay cycle.

HOW TO ANALYSE YOUR SPENDING

Far too many people see the task of analysing their spending as too hard and downright boring. Sure, it can be like that. However, never forget that this is your money and your life you're dealing with. You can choose to do nothing, stay in the pay-to-pay cycle and never get ahead or make a concerted effort and end up living the life you want to live. All it takes is some time away from the TV perhaps to analyse your expenditure. Whenever I used to work with a client in my financial planning practice, I would always ask the following question as a bit of fun before we started analysing their budget.

Which would you prefer? Your money controlling you, or you controlling your money?

Strangely, this question always had a motivational effect!

Analysing your expenses is going to require you to look carefully into your Money Tracker and Category Expenses template looking for opportunities to adjust your spending. I'm not going to spend too much time on this now as you'll find out how to do this in Chapter 4. However, I will say one thing, you need to look very carefully at your fixed expenses first.

A few changes to them (consolidating your loans into one lower rate loan, for example) could end up saving you thousands a year. My suggestion is to look for the big-ticket areas where you could perhaps save in the first instance, then continue the trimming as you move to the variable expenses.

This is exactly what companies do when they look at their Profit and Loss figures. You need to think like a company, look for areas that are costing the most and find ways to trim them first. Small percentage savings from large amounts obviously add up. The moral to the story here is to look for the areas where you have the greatest expenditure and see if you can reduce it by whatever means. Again, look in Chapter 4 for many more ways to adjust your spending.

YOUR TWELVE-MONTH CASH FLOW PICTURE

Now that you've had a chance to look at your expenditure and income patterns from a monthly perspective (courtesy of your Money Tracker and Category Expenses templates) you can easily project and evaluate your money for a twelve-month period.

Once again, hop onto my website <www.budgetblitz.com.au> and download my Cash Flow Planner to make this process much easier. It's an Excel spreadsheet that you can enter your details into as you please with all the formulas and fancy graphs built in.

This will come in handy when you start to look for ways to curb your spending in Chapter 4. You can use my planner in two ways. First, use it as a watchful eye by simply entering information under the categories listed in the spreadsheet using the figures you've established from your Money Tracker and Category Expenses templates. (Note you'll have to spend perhaps an hour or two going through your Money Tracker transferring all the category data into your Budget Planner to set it up.)

To make things easy I have used the same category headings you'll find in the Money Tracker and Category Expenses templates, plus I have added a number of subcategories to help you really break down your expenditure items). Once you've done this and put the same figures in all the monthly columns, you'll need to remember these figures are an averaged set of numbers that you can use to monitor your actual monthly expenditure.

While this approach doesn't require you to consistently enter actual figures it does require you to cast your eye over what's coming in and going out on a monthly basis. In other words, you've got to pay a bit more attention to your bills and statements when you are paying them.

"You should be able to quickly react to a big change in one of your expenditure categories."

This is kind of a relatively low maintenance approach (after the initial set up at least) as it should only take you at most twenty minutes a month to look over your expenses and budget. That's less than an episode of your favourite TV show.

With this heightened awareness, you should be able to quickly react to a big change to one of your expenditure categories and be ready to adjust your spending for the next month.

The second way you can use my Budget Planner is as an ongoing spending tracking tool. In this way you can use it to physically add in how much you spend for each item listed in the spreadsheet in each column for the month.

It's another big ask, I know, but by following this approach you'll get a pretty good grip of what your money situation is doing on a month-to-month basis. This requires you to be vigilant in keeping your spreadsheet updated each month and to have your eyes constantly peeled for any extra activities in your money world. With this approach you will literally have to enter all your expenses and income for that month, either as they come in or at the end of the month. (Don't worry about calculations as the spreadsheet does them automatically.)

By doing this you'll get a pretty accurate indicator of how you are performing each month, as the spreadsheet will show you (like it or not!) whether you are in a surplus or deficit position (that is, profit or loss). To do justice to this approach you will need to spend at least a good hour or two per month. Yes, it will be a right old pain in the you-know-what, but if you want to break out of the pay-to-pay cycle and live the life you want, you will need to put in maximum effort.

In its purest sense, your budget tracks every item in your life, and everything you do in your life. Therefore, it is important you invest the time in completing it.

My dad is a great example of the spending tracking tool approach. He has done this ever since he set up his own businesses in the early 1960s. For many years, he's put together his P and L (as he calls it) for Mum and himself.

While his system may be a little different, and perhaps a little less flash than mine, it is nevertheless on a spreadsheet he created. Not bad for an eighty-six year old! He's been doing this for years and spends a good few hours a month working out his monthly P and L. Okay, you're probably saying he's retired and has got plenty of time on his hands. Not at all; with a mum like mine he's busier than he was when he was working. If it's not playing golf, they're going to Rotary functions or helping out the local church. What's impressive about him (other than being my dad) is he always knows with such accuracy how much they spend and how much they earn (by the way, he also has a self-managed super fund). In fact, his accountant is always blown away when Dad brings in his figures for his annual tax return. He says my dad should set up a business teaching people how to budget!

Speaking of which, I have a very good colleague of mine called David Wright who does that. He's from Queensland and holds seminars across Australia on budgeting. Plus, he has a brilliant software product called Simply Budgets. If you want to really get involved in budgets, I can't speak more highly of him and his product. Want to know more? Check out his website <www.simplybudgets.com.au>.

I'm not precious about what format or template you use when it comes to a budget planner, so I won't be offended if you don't use mine. I encourage you to create your own if you want to, or adapt mine.

At the end of the day, all I wish is that you start to put together a budget (call it spending planner, cash flow manager, or whatever) so that you can track your income and expenses and, ultimately, manage the differences properly.

I just want to see a reversal of the trend of my latest survey into budgeting, where I found that 65 per cent of Australians didn't have a budget in any shape or form, and 14 per cent had one in their head. That left only a very small 21 per cent who had a budget in a written form.

Which category do you fall into?

COPING WITH FLUCTUATIONS IN YOUR INCOME AND EXPENSES

Things will always come up to compete for your attention. For example, over time you'll get pay rises, unexpected bills, buy things on impulse, lose your job, split up with your partner, get a partner, get married, have a baby and so on. Whilst some of these you can predict, others ... well, let's just say they are in the lap of the gods. So rather than being left exposed, I thought I would share with you a few ideas on coping with these potential budget blower-outers!

1. COPING WITH PAY RISES

Not a bad one to have, however in a COVID-19 and post COVID-19 environment chances are slim. But if you are lucky enough to get one, then include that in your income but immediately take out the difference and place it aside in a savings account and call it starter money. You will see what I mean in Chapter 5.

2. BUYING THINGS ON IMPULSE

How do I say this nicely ... DON'T DO IT! You are never going to break out of the pay-to-pay cycle if you continue to buy things without first thinking if you really need them or, more importantly, if you can afford them. Now I want you to raise your right hand and repeat after me, "I promise not to buy anything on impulse for at least the next six months or until I get out of the pay-to-pay cycle". Be gone spending demons!

3. SPLITTING UP WITH YOUR PARTNER

Boy do I have experience here! This can create a huge hole in your budget as well in your assets. The trick is to not let the emotions take hold and partake in too much retail therapy. By all means get the emotions out of your system, but don't end up having double the pain when you get your credit card statement a month later.

4. LOSING YOUR JOB

This one hurts. If you are lucky enough to walk away with a redundancy payment you will need to allocate enough of it to cover your normal expenses for a minimum of a month. Being your pseudo-income for the time it takes you to get a new job, your redundancy payment should be treated as income. Avoid doing some retail therapy. Depending on the amount you receive and how long it will take to get another job, you'll need every dollar. If you are lucky enough to get a job quickly then, sure, have some fun, but also think about reducing debts and perhaps investing some. (I cover more on this in Chapters 5 and 7.)

BASIC MONEY MANAGEMENT SKILLS FOR KIDS

Quick question: How different would your finances be today if you were taught more about money when you were young?

Think about it for a moment. Were you taught basic money skills at school or by your parents?

While you are thinking about that, here's some alarming statistics from a recent survey I conducted into Kids, Money and Adult financial literacy. Alarmingly, of the 1,500 Australians who participated, more than six out of 10 (62 per cent) who rated themselves as poor money handlers were not taught about money as children. What's even scarier is that of that 62 per cent, 78 per cent of them believe that they are passing on bad financial habits to their children.

Luckily, I had a pretty good set of teachers in my parents, but when it came to school all I can remember learning about money is the nice man from the bank visiting the school each week, giving us pencils and collecting the money from our passbooks.

The school curriculum back then just didn't cut it. Nowadays there's some great work with financial literacy becoming part of the curriculum, with many schools implementing programs. However, I still believe there is a huge gap in money education that needs to be filled.

If you are a parent, I believe it is your responsibility to teach your children. I can go on for hours talking about how and when to teach your children about money, but I won't. When it comes to teaching kids the fundamentals, all I can suggest is you teach them how to compartmentalise their money. Get them to allocate any money they receive for Christmas or birthdays or as pocket money and so on, into four distinct areas:

1. Giving (giving money to charity)

2. Living (day-to-day living and buying things)

3. Saving (money to be saved up for short-term things like a new computer game, bike or toy)

4. Investing (money to be saved in a high interest bank account for later on)

Applying this system can be amazingly simple. Imagine your child gets $100 from their granny for Christmas. Instead of putting it straight into the bank or spending it, you give them the option of how they want to allocate it. Obviously you may need to coach them a little, but they will eventually get the hang of it.

Granted, these four areas are pretty simple, but when you think about it, that's pretty much all they need to start their young minds off. Making it easy to follow and understand by using the four-compartment approach should remain with them well into their adulthood.

In fact, when they get the chance to do their own budget later on, their basic training with the Giving, Living, Saving and Investing approach will pay off. Best of all, they will not be afraid of money allocation or budgeting.

STICK TO THE BASICS

The secret to financial freedom does not reside in sophisticated investment strategies. It starts with getting the fundamentals right. That is, you need to understand where your money is coming from and where it is going. Know how to pay yourself first and the rest will follow. I think too many of us view all this money stuff as far too complicated and think it must require a complicated solution.

The reality cannot be further from the truth. It's simply a matter of getting your cash flows under control and getting the basics right. Sure, it may require a bit of time and commitment on your behalf, but let me reassure you, it's not rocket science.

Before I move onto the next chapter, let me share with you a story about focusing on the basics. A few years back I was asked to present at a forum of "investors" in Sydney. There were about three thousand people who had paid about $5,000 each to come along. I prepared my forty-five minute presentation according to the brief and arrived early just to hear the other speakers ahead of me. What I heard made me quake in my boots. Every presenter was talking about sophisticated options, futures and hedging strategies. Not that there is anything wrong with that, but my brief was to talk about simple cash flow management techniques and pitch it at an entry level.

My high noon arrived and before I knew it, I was being ushered to a dark stage. Then lights up and ... silence.

I couldn't help thinking, "Run Forest Run!" Even the Options presenter was greeted with a huge round of applause. For me, silence.

I have to say, I was petrified. Don't get me wrong, I had done literally hundreds of these types of presentations before, but for some reason I thought I wasn't going to be sophisticated enough and I'd be booed off the stage. I really had to muster all my courage. I must say, it was the longest forty-five minutes of my life.

When I finished, I drew a deep breath and thanked the audience. Deathly silence. Not even a clap. Oh, that's it, I thought. Beam me up Scotty! NOW!

But after what seemed to be minutes (in fact was only milliseconds), the whole audience rose and gave me a standing ovation. I thought they were humouring me, but then the weirdest thing happened. Literally hundreds of those people who were standing came running toward the stage. All of them wanted to thank me for delivering the most insightful presentation of the day.

I was mobbed. I couldn't believe what I was hearing, as nearly all of them said I had woken them up to the need to get their basic budgeting and cash flow fundamentals right before they embarked on any advanced strategies.

The options and futures guys weren't that happy with me, and neither was the event organiser as hardly any of the attendees signed up for their "sophisticated investor programs" on the spot as they would have hoped.

I sold over 2,000 copies of this book (in its previous edition) that day alone.

The message to me was don't over complicate things. Make them relatable and make them simple.

Now for the next few chapters that will help you understand the power of cash flow management.

CHAPTER 4
IT'S TIME TO CHANGE YOUR SPENDING HABITS

Now that you know how much you spend, thanks to the last chapter, here comes the part where you have to take a serious look at your spending habits. In this chapter I'm going to present to you a series of questions and templates that will help you focus on your spending habits. To make it real, I thought I'd share with you a story of how I coped with being dumped into the pay-to-pay cycle and what actions I took to get myself out.

Let me warn you. Some of the things you are about to read in this chapter are going to sound quite simple, and you'll find yourself saying "Yeah, I knew that" a fair bit. But as you do, can I encourage you to ask yourself the question: Do I actually do that? I'm sure you'll find some interesting answers along the way.

Before I get stuck into ways to change your spending habits, I'd like to have a quick chat about your spending mindset and take a look at how it impacts your day-to-day life and, of course, your budget.

THE 7 SPENDING MINDSETS

When it comes to spending habits, I have identified seven different mindsets that are constantly playing out in your head. While each one gets a turn at affecting you in some way or another, they all impact differently on the amount of money you end up spending and, ultimately, how much you have left over between pays. Understanding them holds the key to changing your spending habits, as they will impact your conscious and subconscious behaviour when it comes to your overall handling of your money.

1. THE DRUNKEN SAILOR

You will have the tendency to spend whatever extra cash you have, even if you have major debts that could be paid down faster. Sometimes this mindset manifests in a whimsical spending spree which can cause a massive credit card hangover later on.

2. THE ENTERTAINER

Spending money is like a form of entertainment to you. As long as you are spending you are happy. Unfortunately, too much of this happiness creates a potential debt problem as you rack up the old credit card.

3. THE THERAPIST

Like everyone, from time to time, and for a multitude of reasons, you find yourself in peaks and troughs of emotions. As a result you respond by perhaps treating yourself to a little retail therapy. Whether you are happy or sad, you still end up spending money that you may in fact regret spending once the emotions settle.

4. BARGAIN BETTY

You clearly have a nose for spotting a bargain and have a definite knack for getting the best deal in town. You buy well and spend wisely. There is, however, a fine line between savvy spending and a shopaholic, as a bargain is not a bargain unless you actually need what you are buying.

5. GREEDY GRABBER

Just because your neighbours have got something doesn't necessarily mean that you should have the same, or better. Because of the massive pressures from our "Got to have it now" culture, you end up buying a number of things that you may not even need. The more you spend, the more financial envy grows amongst your friends and family, and the more pressure you put on your finances in keeping up with everyone else.

6. THE PINCHER

You watch every cent you spend like a hawk and sometimes you can go to extremes just to not spend money. Keeping a close eye on your money is one thing, but being obsessed about it is clearly another.

7. CLEVER COOKIE

You have a pretty good handle on how to spend your money wisely. Well, perhaps not all the time (you are human after all), but on the whole you show quite a good aptitude in knowing how to plan your spending and negotiate a deal.

Which one do you think you are? Chances are, like your overall money personality, you are made up of parts of the above. However, there is a strong probability that one or other is dominant at any points in your life. This is quite normal, but you should always aim to try and move your spending mindset toward the Clever Cookie, as this will help you manage your spending in such a way that you can still enjoy life without creating huge debt consequences.

HOW TO IMPROVE YOUR SPENDING HABITS

Understand your mindset and you are halfway there. Identify a few things you can do to make a change and you're three-quarters of the way there. Put them into action and you're well on your way to making a significant change. Speaking of which, here's a few things you can do straight away to improve each of the seven mindsets:

1. THE DRUNKEN SAILOR

To change this mindset you simply need to curb your urge to splurge. Just use what I call the "Spending Reality Checker", where you divide the cost of the item you wish to buy by your hourly rate. Here you'll get a figure that represents the number of hours you need to work in order to buy that item! As the name suggests, it's a great reality checker.

2. THE ENTERTAINER

If this is your dominant mindset you need to change your consumption habits; instead of focusing on buying things you focus on buying things you need. Shopping is not a sport.

3. THE THERAPIST

When you are in an emotional state, it's best if you simply refrain from buying anything. If you have to shop, ask a friend to help. Having them there will be the best leveller you can get. Whatever you do, never shop with a person who has a similar emotionally charged mindset ... it will be like the blind leading the blind.

4. BARGAIN BETTY

Compare notes with other savvy shoppers and learn from their advice. Always remember, someone, somewhere has a great tip on how to get better value. If you want to improve just listen to them. For those Bargain Bettys who are close to shopaholics, always ask yourself the question "Do I really need this?" before you score the deal of a lifetime. If that's not enough, perhaps perform the Spending Reality Checker in your head.

5. GREEDY GRABBER

Start by curbing your financial envy. You have to forget about the Joneses and get the "got to have it now" mentality out of your head. Try and refocus your spending from extravagant items to saving up for them first; you'll definitely appreciate them more. Perhaps you could even use the good old lay-by system!

6. THE PINCHER

If this is your mindset you need to learn to live a little. By all means keep up the good work of maintaining a close eye on your financials, but never get too tight with your money. A little enjoyment can go a long way and give you a really positive mindset for other areas in your life.

7. CLEVER COOKIE

Despite this being the mindset you should be aspiring to, it still can be improved. A constant refinement of your spending patterns through smarter negotiation techniques will help you continually reduce your expense items. The key here is to keep your mindset focused on reducing expenses, maximising value and enjoying life without the worry of debt all at the same time.

Please remember that, like your money personality, your core spending mindset has probably taken your whole lifetime to develop, so go easy on the changes. Try implementing some of the methods mentioned above, but be aware that making too many changes too quickly won't work. You can't change your core traits overnight. Nevertheless, don't give up trying to change.

PUTTING THESE CHANGES INTO ACTION

Rather than give you some boring old theory on how to change your spending habits, I thought I'd share with you what happened to me a few years back when I found myself smack in the middle of the pay-to-pay cycle ... literally overnight. Here, I'm going to candidly share with you what happened, what I had to do to rectify the situation and how my mindset was affected.

June 17 2003 is a day I'll never forget as long as I live. At about 10.30 am, I answered a call from my accountant who, within the first thirty seconds, gave me some very grave news. In a sombre voice he told me I'd have to shut one of my key businesses (the Money Café centres) because they were bleeding so much cash he didn't expect them to make it to the end of the financial year.

I'd expected the call, but secretly hoped it would never come. This was definitely not the kind of news I wanted to hear, especially since I was still laid flat on my back with a weird mystery illness. Unfortunately, the reality of the situation was my income was far less than my expenses and the business was dipping into my ever-dwindling personal cash reserves at an incredible rate. I needed to cut back on my spending fast.

Sure, I had very good records, but that doesn't help you when the losses keep mounting. Looking back, having these records was a good thing – they provided an early warning system for my accountant. Unfortunately, in the personal budgeting world, as we discovered in Chapter 3, not everybody has a budget for their personal finances, so predicting potential problems is not easy. This is one of the reasons we go from problem to problem and stay in the pay-to-pay cycle.

"Not everybody has a budget for their personal finances, so predicting potential problems is not easy."

Luckily, I used the spreadsheet I spoke about in Chapter 3 to create a set of pie charts to help me identify the areas where I was spending the most. When you see it in a picture it takes on a whole new meaning. I suggest you give this a go (if you've not already done so) as I'm sure you will be surprised with what percentage your expenses take of your total income. In the financial world, this ratio is called the expenditure ratio (where you simply divide your total income by your total expenses to reveal a percentage).

Interestingly, the average income to expense ratio last year across Australia was 150 per cent, which means that for every $100 earned, $200 was spent. (I mentioned this in Chapter 1.)

No wonder debts are rising exponentially, as the money has to come from somewhere. There are really no hard and fast rules when it comes to what your expenditure ratio should be, but clearly the lower you get it the more profitable you will be. It's a great measure to know.

THE TOUGH QUESTIONS

Back to my story ...

Rather than going bankrupt, my accountant asked me during that same phone call if I was prepared to answer some pretty hard questions and then to do whatever was required to curb my expenses. Even though we were talking about my business, the questions he asked me can be applied to anyone in any situation.

To show you what I mean, here are the questions my accountant posed, and some of the answers – plus actions – I took. I'm sure, like me, you know the questions and kind of have the answers. But sometimes reality is hard to face, so you end up sweeping them under the carpet and hoping they will go away.

Unfortunately, they won't. My accountant's objective here was quite simple. Control the costs, get the business on an even keel and sell it for whatever we could get before it dragged me down further. By the way, all of the actions I applied to my business I also applied to my personal life, as my personal finances were also incredibly badly affected by this whole ordeal. At that stage I was beyond the pay-to-pay cycle as I had absolutely no personal income coming in! Very much like millions of Australian right now as a result of COVID-19.

While some of my answers and actions may be relevant to you, I do encourage you to ask yourself the same questions when you're reading this, to see if you can come up with a set of answers and actions to change or improve your own spending habits.

QUESTION ONE: can you get by with less sophisticated and less expensive things?

This was a lot easier to do for my business than in my personal life, as in my business I could make these decisions with far less emotion involved. The first thing I did was look at all my expenses (both for the business and for my personal life) and list them from the most expensive to the least (having this information at my fingertips made it all very easy).

Then, starting at the most expensive item, I made a note as to whether it was absolutely necessary. If it wasn't, it had to go. Sure, it was a ruthless decision, but I was on a mission to cut expenses rapidly. Next, I looked at what was left on the list and worked out if I could replace it with a less expensive version.

It's kind of strange when you actually do this. Even though you know that sometimes a brand name doesn't necessarily mean value for money, you can get caught up in the hype. For my coffee shop (the Money Café), the first thing I changed was the brand of coffee. Instead of using the expensive leading brand, I switched to an unknown brand that was a fraction of the cost. Amazingly, our customers loved the new taste.

When it came to cutting back on personal expenses, I had to go through a bit of an emotional challenge. Because times were pretty good until then, I was used to having the latest and greatest gadgets. And, yes, I admit I was a bit of a Greedy Grabber.

Because of my situation I had to make a number of hard sacrifices. Rather than getting depressed about it and thinking I was a failure, I took it in my stride. (I suggest, if you find yourself in a similar situation you do the same. I can't stress enough the need for maintaining your confidence through what may seem to be devastatingly hard times.)

I knew deep down this was only a short-term measure, but it was absolutely necessary to get me out of the predicament I was in. Knowing what I had to do, I took a deep breath and walked through my home with a notepad listing things that I clearly didn't need ... or in fact ever used. I'm sure you've got the same in your home – things that look good, and are good bragging material – but let's face it, keeping up with the Joneses is not relevant, particularly when you are in a situation like mine.

Unfortunately, I had fallen prey to the consumer world, with my flat screen TV, entertainment systems and other whiz-bang household gadgets. It was now a matter of pruning for regrowth!

To get some extra cash, I sold many things in my apartment that I really didn't need. Then, to save some dollars, I scaled down where I lived and moved to a less expensive unit. At the end of all this realignment and downsizing, I realised my life was just the same – only cheaper and less stressful, and I had more money in my pocket.

If your personal situation is anything like mine was, and you're really struggling for day-to-day cash, I suggest you take a very close look at your Cash Flow Planner template (remember Chapter 3) and consider getting rid of some of your luxuries, like alcohol, ring tones on your mobile, cable TV, magazine subscriptions, cigarettes and music downloads.

Look at any habit you have and work out how much it costs you each year. You may even want to take a look at the 28 Day Budget Blitz at <Budgetblitz.com.au> where you can find ways to cut back but still live a good life and also generate a cool $20,000 in annual savings by doing a few things smarter. Check it out.

As you can see, there are plenty of ways you can get by with less sophisticated and less expensive things, and I've only covered a mere few. Have a go for yourself and see what you can come up with using the spending template below. (Please note that this is a generic template and yours will definitely vary, so don't be afraid to add and subtract whatever's appropriate.)

Start with the Expense categories from the Category Expenses template in Chapter 3. Then add in more specific items for each category. (As you can see below, for Housing you can add in Rent or Mortgage, for example.) Then put in a Y or N, noting whether it is necessary or not.

For each Expense item, outline how you will go about making it less sophisticated or less expensive, and then make an estimate of how much you should potentially save by doing this. This will give you a much clearer picture of which expenses you should be spending most of your time on. Always focus on the ones that you can save the most money on first. As an example, remember when I had to relocate to a less expensive unit? There were big savings there. If moving isn't an option, you could consider renting out a room to a roommate or relative. Obviously, this isn't an ideal situation for the long-term, but keep telling yourself that it's only temporary. Let's say you get $300 a month by doing this, which is $1,800 over a six-month period. That's more than half of the average credit card balance of $3,231. See this stuff really adds up.

MY SPENDING CHECKER

Category Expense	Expense Item	Is it Necessary?	What can you do to make it less sophisticated and/or less expensive?	Potential $ Savings
Housing	Rent			
Housing	Mortgage			
Insurance				
Health/Medical				
Housing Maintenance				
Utilities and telecommunications				
Transport				
Food				
Clothes				
Education				
Personal (alcohol, cigarettes)				
Hobbies/Sport				
Holidays				
Gifts				
Pets				
Repayments (personal loans, credit cards)				
Total Savings				$

(Again, this template is also available to download from <www.budgetblitz.com.au>).

QUESTION TWO: Are you using more of the products or services you receive than you really need?

Two words came into my head when my accountant asked this question – excess consumption. (Not just the ones you were probably thinking of.) I guess we are all guilty of this in some way or another. The trick is to recognise it.

Unfortunately, it's very hard to in this day and age where we seem to live in such a consumer-oriented society. When I looked at my business, I very quickly found about ten areas where we were using much more than we needed. For example, we had too many staff working in shifts that had small customer traffic; we would consistently over-order cakes and pastries; we left the lights on during the night; we had an internet service that was ten times the capacity we needed, and so on. You might be saying to yourself, "Yikes, he calls himself a sharp businessman". Well, it's amazing how these little cost overruns can become quite large, especially if there is no eagle eye watching over them. Unfortunately, as I was laid low over three months, these costs simply blew right out as there was no-one there to call the shots.

On the personal side I then had to look very closely into the main areas where I spent my money to see if I, too, was over-consuming. I looked at all the areas where I spent my money and addressed them one by one, starting with my housing. As I mentioned above, I had downsized my home and was now in a much cheaper one, so I was okay there.

At that stage my fiancée was living with me and we both had big appetites, which made it difficult to cut back on food. We did, however, make simple adjustments to the way we bought fruit and vegetables, for example, so that they could last longer. We bought things like bananas at various stages of ripening so that as the week went by we'd have plenty of fruit and not end up throwing any away. I know this is simple stuff, but it is the key to adjusting your spending. We certainly didn't go without, we simply bought smarter. Here our mindset, as you can see, was quite the Clever Cookie.

With our clothing we found that we had far too much, especially my fiancée. (I don't know how many pairs of shoes one person can have, but at $200 a pop it all adds up.) I must confess I had my own shopping weakness and that was for shirts. I can't explain it, but I loved to buy really nice casual or business shirts. The only problem was I had too many of them, and ended up only wearing them once or twice. (By the time the next fashions had come, in I'd relegate them to the back of my wardrobe.)

Curbing the clothing excess was a pretty easy adjustment for both of us, as we were in it together. This is a good lesson to learn: have the support and encouragement of each other. Without it, fights and other problems occur. All through this experience we kept reminding ourselves that this was only for the short term.

"I guess we are all guilty of excess consumption in some way or another. The trick is to recognise it."

Instead of clothes shopping every month, we reduced the number of items we bought, plus reduced the number of times we went shopping for clothes. Essentially we now bought at discount factory outlets or at sales. I still do this and manage to get some really great stuff for a fraction of the price. Although post COVID-19 I'm now buying online, hunting deals, shopping all over the world and saving a bundle when I shop.

Next on my list was our entertainment expenditure. I'm going to sound like a real scrooge when it comes to what I did, but the tough times called for it. The bottom line was our eating-out budget was huge. I can understand it for the three months when I was sick, as it was hard to share the cooking load at home given that I was pretty much useless and my fiancée was always working late at her job to support us. But when I looked closely at it, we didn't eat it all then and there and were wasting a lot of money. So a plan was drawn up to make some cutbacks. Again, we both knew that this wasn't forever, so it kept us motivated as we still really enjoyed the convenience and taste of eating out.

Our approach was quite simple: we cooked at home more (it became great therapy for me, I might add) and we used the discount vouchers we got from the Entertainment Book we had lying around. Now the Bargain Betty mindset kicked in.

At the end of the day, all of the things I had to do to cut back on my expenses on both a business and personal level were really quite simple. All it took was a kind of re-awakening to do more of the basic things.

I had put a number of them into action before, but this was the first time I'd ever put them all into play at the same time. It was quite an amazing experience. At the end of it I saw a huge change in the amount of money left over after all my expenses.

I guess we all know a number of these ways of getting the most for our dollar, but sometimes in the pursuit of getting out of the pay-to-pay cycle we tend to overcomplicate the solutions and look for more sophisticated answers. It really is very simple. Forget searching for technical solutions and focus on the basics.

Nothing really ever happens if you don't write it down, so here's yet another template (sorry, I do love them) to help you get more value for money across all your expenses. Have a go at it. Start by jotting down the expense categories you feel you are over-indulging on. Then write down some ideas on how you are going to cut back on the expenses. (Think about when I cut back on clothes and entertainment.)

Several ways to cut back will come to you if you keep thinking about it. Here's a hint: just like a Clever Cookie, ask your friends and your family if they have any little money-saving ideas that they follow. You're bound to find a lot. If you're still stuck, hop onto my website <www.budgetblitz.com.au> and invest in the 28 Day Budget Blitz. I can guarantee it can cut your spending by up to $10,000 a year. Yep, that's right. In fact, if you can't save at least the $20 you spent I'll gladly refund you.

In the final column have a go at estimating how much you may save by putting into action what you've said in the "Ideas to cut back on excesses" column. By doing this it will really show you how much you are currently wasting, and what amount of money you could have left over after your expenses ... if you only managed your spending habits better.

Category Expense	Expense Item	Is it Necessary?	What can you do to make it less sophisticated and / or less expensive?	Potential $ Savings
Housing	Rent			
Housing	Mortgage			
Insurance				
Health/Medical				
Housing Maintenance				
Utilities and telecommunications				
Transport				
Food				
Clothes				
Education				
Personal (alcohol, cigarettes etc)				
Hobbies/Sport				
Holidays				
Gifts				
Pets				
Repayments (personal loans, credit cards)				
Total Savings				$

QUESTION THREE: are you buying things at a competitive price?

How often do you ask for a discount when you are buying things? If the answer is "always", quickly skip read this section. However, if you said "not often" or "never", read this very carefully as you will be able to save many thousands per year by putting into action some of these ideas.

The simple art of negotiation goes a long way.

One of the great things my boss at the stock exchange taught me was how not to pay full price. He was an amazing bloke and had this uncanny knack of never paying full price for just about anything, ranging from cars to things around the home – even with his solicitor (now that was a good one!). His approach was quite straightforward and consisted of five simple rules:

1. Do your homework on what you want to buy: check out at least five competitors and note how much each of them have the item listed for. By doing your homework you'll end up with a good understanding of what you are actually getting for your money and, in doing so, you may also find out what other things you could possibly get thrown in when it comes to finalising the deal.

2. Get your timing right: mid-year and end-of-year sales are clearly good times to buy things at a lower price, however there are other times of the year when you can also get great deals. They are toward the end of the month or the end of the quarter. For many retailers, these points on the calendar represent key milestones in terms of sales targets. Therefore, if you strike then you may be able to get a pretty good deal. This is especially true if you are shopping for a car, for instance.

3. Always ask for a better price: whatever some people say, asking for a better price should not be considered embarrassing. Always remind yourself that it's your money you're spending so the objective is to spend it as wisely as you can.

If this requires you to ask for a better price, then do so. Never forget that you are the one in the power position in any negotiation when you are the buyer. If you get a better price it means more money in your pocket. This is particularly handy if you are struggling to get out of the pay-to-pay cycle. Now I can see that you may be a little sceptical here, but let me give you an example to prove my point. Let's take the good old credit card. Did you know that all you have to do is call up your current credit card company and say you are thinking of leaving them and getting a different credit card with a lower rate? Ask them point blank if they can do better. Granted, some cards won't budge. Many others will, so you could be pleasantly surprised.

1. Be confident: when you're negotiating you'll need to exude an air of confidence so that you maintain control. But whatever you do, try not to come across as being arrogant – that won't get you anywhere. When you ask for a deal or a better price, be firm with your request and be prepared to ask the person you're dealing with a second time. Salespeople all over the world (from retailers to business development managers for professional service companies) are highly trained to deal with customers. They figure if they say no to an initial request there's a great probability the person won't ask again. But not you after reading this book, hey? Sometimes you may even need to have enough confidence to politely ask if you can see the manager to negotiate with them. When you're doing this, try to not belittle the person you are initially negotiating with, as you still want them on your side when the boss comes around. Finally, be prepared to walk if the deal is not what you want. If you have done your homework and have some alternative suppliers, have the confidence to take your business elsewhere.

2. Close the deal on your terms: once you've reached an agreement, get the deal in writing. That way you will always have proof of the negotiation. Then conclude with the payment terms if there is an opportunity.

These rules came in handy when I had to evaluate my business expenses. Luckily, I had been paying close attention to what my manager had taught me all those years ago. My Bargain Betty mindset was strong when I was setting up the Money Café, so I managed to secure some pretty competitive deals, ranging from a good rental agreement, to good negotiated salaries for management staff.

"My Bargain Betty mindset was strong, so I managed to secure some pretty competitive deals."

I must admit, when my back was against the wall, I found this extra drive to squeeze a little harder. Even though you may think you have done well, there's always a little more you can save. Let's face it, that money is far better off in your pocket than anyone else's!

So how are you going so far?

Making sense?

I hope you can see how it fits together when you view it through the life of someone else.

My challenge to you, is to see if you can make a list of the areas of expense in your life (no templates this time!) where you can get more price competitive.

For example, you may have a home loan, a personal loan and one or more credit cards. All you need to do is shop around for the best deal and then see if you can consolidate your debts into the one loan. (You can get a mortgage broker to do the shopping around – they are free and do all the leg work for you.) This will save you a massive amount of money and you will only have one loan at a much lower interest rate. The only trick here is that you need to make a few extra payments with the money you now have left over each month to pay down this new loan as fast as you can. Why? It's simple: if you have consolidated your credit cards and personal loan (which are generally short-term loans) into a thirty-year home loan, you may be effectively paying off last week's Chinese takeaway for a long time. Hence the reason to make extra payments. (I'll cover more of this in the next chapter.) If you don't have a home loan, you can still take advantage of cheap credit cards that offer zero balance transfers.

You see what I mean?

So now simply list the three areas of your expenses where you could potentially use the five steps to negotiate the best price:

1. ______________________________

2. ______________________________

3. ______________________________

QUESTION FOUR: Are you spending too much money relative to your income, and are there any other opportunities for you to save?

Given the amount of income for both the business and what I was receiving personally, this question was pretty easy to answer. Even though I thought I'd done a good job putting into place various actions to stem the outflows of cash, I was still in a negative cash flow position businesswise and personally. Being in this situation can topple a business or put a person in bankruptcy – I certainly didn't want either to happen.

My ever-vigilant accountant then asked whether I had in fact looked at every single opportunity to save money. Honestly, I felt like I was in a juicer and it was turned on high. How much more could he squeeze out of me? I already had the Bargain Betty and Clever Cookie mindsets working in overdrive so I was bound to get the best deals across the board. However, this was not good enough for him.

I thought long and hard about this and then ... Eureka! Why not look deeper into those bundling discounts offered with things like my insurances, telephone, utility bills and banking products.

This turned out to be a great thought – I simply called them up and asked if there were any extra benefits that I wasn't actually getting. Surprisingly, I got further discounts on my telephone and utility bills and on my banking products. Interestingly, all of these extra discounts were brand new and hadn't made it to the market. That's a lesson in itself, and I suggest you call up your utility, phone and internet, banking and insurance companies to see if these bundling discounts apply. Granted, you may not see some of the impacts immediately (except with your phone and internet), but over the year they add up. Again, the Bargain Betty mindset to the rescue.

QUESTION FIVE: Are you jeopardising your financial future with your current spending habits?

This is a long story, I know, but hopefully one you are learning something from. In 2003 I was staring down the very ugly barrel of business and personal bankruptcy. Even though you'd think that you probably need a Drunken Sailor or Entertainer mindset to get in that position, sometimes unfortunate circumstances take you there. You may not have experienced a time that has set you back like that, but if you are in the pay-to-pay cycle and want to get out, similar rules apply.

My financial future didn't look good. I had two options in front of me that were almost as bad as each other. The first was to declare myself bankrupt, the second to attempt to trade out. I certainly didn't like the stigma attached with bankruptcy, nor its limitations. So that only left me with the option of trading out. This involved even more cost-cutting. (You'd be surprised what you can find when you are that motivated.) I was a little cheeky here and created a third option: sell the business. Unfortunately, I was only going to get a very small fraction of what it was potentially worth, but who's going to pay top dollar for a thing that's come through some rough times, even if it has got plenty of potential? To cut a long story short, I sold it and closed that chapter in my life. It was hard to let go after all the blood sweat and tears I'd put into it, but better to end a bad situation before it gets any worse.

I thank my accountant for giving me his five questions and for providing the focus to do what I had to do. My habits needed sharpening and I am very grateful to him for helping me here.

Now, I hear you saying, well that's all great Greg. You had professional help and I don't. Remember, all my accountant did was pose the questions. I had the records (the budget) and I came up with all the ways to cut my expenses.

That's why I've spent so much time in this Chapter sharing these questions with you, so you can have the same start I did.

When COVID-19 arrived, it delivered a crushing blow to a few of my businesses, effectively wiping out their revenue. I didn't panic.

It was like I was on autopilot, calmly and following the checklist I spoke about in Chapters 3 and 4. Once you do this it becomes second nature and you are able to respond better to any Money Monsters that cross your path.

WHERE TO FROM HERE?

You may not be comfortable bargaining and squeezing the most out of every dollar. But let me remind you that if you are in the pay-to-pay cycle and in a deficit position (worked out from your planner in Chapter 3), you need to make some changes.

Fast.

Start by getting a handle on your money mindset (you saw mine ranged from being a Clever Cookie to a Greedy Grabber to a Bargain Betty). Luckily, I held my positive attitude throughout all of this, and I didn't slip into the Therapist mindset.

Your mindset will change over time; I encourage you to discover what it is now, and how you can make the improvements so that you can ultimately become a Clever Cookie. Ask yourself the tough questions, and by all means use the templates I've given you. Keep up your confidence throughout all of this. If you have to make some tough cuts, remember they are short-term. Every cut will bring you closer and closer to busting right out of that pay-to-pay cycle and into a territory that will give you plenty of leftover cash so you can live the life you want to live.

CHAPTER 5
CONTROLLING YOUR DEBTS

I hope by now you've got a pretty good handle on where most of your money is coming from and where it's going.

Unfortunately, for all too many people a great proportion of their money is going to pay off debt. In fact, from a recent survey I did of 1000 people I found that 48 per cent were allocating more than half of their income just to pay back their debts.

With that in mind, I'm going to show you a number of ways to not only reduce your debts faster but crush them in time frames you could only have dreamed of.

But let me start with a set of quick definitions so we can both sing from the same hymn book. Essentially there are two kinds of debt – **good debt** and **bad debt**. Good debt is where you borrow money to acquire an income-producing asset and you use the income that comes from it to pay off your bad debt. You can also claim a tax deduction on the interest bill (more on that later). Bad debt is non-deductible debt, which means you can't get any type of tax deduction. As well, the interest rate (except for home loans) is generally quite high. Examples of bad debt include credit cards, personal loans and in-store credit.

As I mentioned in Chapter 1, far too many Australians have

over-indulged in the past twenty years and have now racked up more than $1 trillion in personal debt. (A little over ten years ago we collectively only owed $425 billion!) Credit cards have also gone through a huge explosion in use. Since late 2000 the amount owing on credit cards has risen from $15.5 billion to a whopping $29 billion. (Source: RBA) That's nearly a 100 per cent increase!

In terms of the average card balance it has grown from $1,504 in 2000 to $3,231 in 2020. That's an increase of 114%. Add to that the exponential growth of the buy now, pay later schemes and the fact that 66% of balances are attracting interest rates of up to 21 per cent per annum, there is little wonder why the credit card debt cycle is vicious.

WORKING OUT HOW MUCH YOU OWE

There are a further two kinds of debt that you encounter on a daily basis – household bills and financial debt. In this chapter I'm only going to refer to financial debt because household bills have to be paid on time to avoid getting your services cut. Therefore, as I discussed in Chapter 4, you should work on ways to get your household bills under control.

Financial debt comes in many forms: credit card, store credit card, buy now, pay later arrangement, personal loan, a loan from a relative or a home loan. You may have some or all of these, but at the end of the day you need to pay close attention to your debt-to-income ratio. In other words, how much you owe relative to your income. This is calculated by dividing your debt by your income. Banks and lenders like you to have a debt-to-income ratio of around 30 to 40 per cent. If your debt-to-income ratio is any higher it means you are in some serious debt and may struggle to pay it back if you need to do so quickly.

When it comes to your debt-to-income ratio your goal should be to reduce the bad debt ratio as fast as you can. I'm shortly going to show you how to do this with my Debt Buster Program.

If you've done your homework properly in Chapter 3, you should have your total debts easily accessible, so you can now start looking at ways of reducing them.

BE CAREFUL WITH THE DEBTS YOU GET YOURSELF INTO IN THE FIRST PLACE

My mum always used to say: "Don't buy it if you can't afford it". A very good piece of advice that I've taken all through my life, especially when it comes to buying big ticket items like buying a home, a car or even furniture.

In her world you had to save up for it and then buy it. Nowadays, with savings being a little more difficult, this is almost impossible. Hence, we need to use loans. I still hear my mum's voice in my head when I'm buying something new or just about to take out a loan. She made pretty good sense here as there's no point in borrowing huge sums of money if you can't pay it back. Sure, sometimes you can make things look good on paper, but that's not going to get you far.

Dad had a different take on debt: he saw it as a way of increasing his assets whilst using someone else's money. He was never afraid of it and used it constantly and, of course, wisely. (Although Mum was always in his ear offering her very conservative advice!) Back in the 1960s, when he was buying a home, there were no mortgage brokers to help him research lenders. Nor were there websites like Finder and RateCity to help him compare features and rates. He had to do all the research himself. (How lucky we are now to have these types of services pretty much at our fingertips, plus a greater choice with the increased number of lenders and products available.)

Dad's key piece of advice to me about debt, which I'd like to pass on to you now, is you need to get the right loan, credit card or whatever to fit your needs. Sure, you need to look for the best price, but sometimes the cheapest product is not the best. Cheap in the financial world nowadays usually means that there are strings attached. You may be able to get a great rate, but there may also be a few catches (like a big annual fee with credit cards, or perhaps a large exit fee with a mortgage).

The bottom line here is, you need to look carefully into what you are getting, and seek the advice of a professional early. If, for example, you are looking for a home loan, always use a mortgage broker. They'll help you with comparing the loans and dealing with the lenders, plus they'll explain the banking jargon and show you the best ways to use offset accounts, redraw facilities, extra repayments, special packages, and so on.

"You need to look carefully into what you are getting, and seek the advice of a professional."

A good broker will spend time with you asking questions that may seem a tad personal, but they are only doing that so they can match the right product to you. The kind of questions they'll ask will include: Are you planning on a family? Are you expecting a pay rise? Do you get bonuses? Do you want to start a business? Have you ever been bankrupt or got a black mark on your credit history? Do you want to invest? Do you want to buy a new car?

The reason why they are doing this is so that they can match your needs with the loan or lender that would be most suitable for you. Because they cover many different lenders, chances are they'll find a loan that's most suitable for your specific circumstances.

Different loan packages will give you different features and benefits, and will come with a different set of rates and fees. Here's where the broker really comes in handy (apart from the fact they don't charge for their services as they get paid by the lender they introduce your loan to).

Use a broker properly. Be as open and honest as you can about what you want to achieve, and I can pretty much guarantee they will find you a better deal than you could find yourself. If you need help in finding a home or investment loan that best suits you, just hop on to my website and I'll point you in the right direction.

With credit cards, check out Finder, RateCity and Mozo, to name a few. Do yourself a favour and spend some time there.

For the likes of Afterpay, Zip, Klarna and so on, be on your guard. Don't rush into signing up for them as they are very good marketers. They may seem awesome on the way in and, if you pay on time, they are good, but the moment you set one foot wrong (miss a repayment), you get slugged with interest of up to 28 per cent per annum (possibly back-dated to the beginning of the contract).

If you are going to sign up for one of these deals, listen out for my little old mum's whisper in your ear ... Do you really need it? Now, don't get me wrong, I'm not saying these deals are bad. In fact, they are brilliant ways to buy something with someone else's money. But be very careful not to let your payments slip. Plus, do not accept their offer for other forms of credit.

It's amazing how many people I see who have got the wrong types of debt, such as having a gold credit card with a frequent flyer program but they don't fly. Why pay for an annual fee and a high interest rate just to have a flashy gold or platinum card. The heady spending days are over folks, and thanks to COVID-19 your number one rule is to get the most basic credit card at the lowest interest rate possible.

It's the same when it comes to home loan packages. When I was a mortgage broker, one of my clients used to be super proud of his "Professional's Package", which had all the bells and whistles such as a discount on the standard variable rate and redraw. Except all he needed was a super low rate loan.

Recently, I bumped into him and asked him how he was. COVID-19 considering he was okay and even mentioned that he still had his Professionals Package. I then said casually that he could simply switch to a lower rate right now and get a better rate. I even pointed out he could potentially save on his monthly repayments and put those savings in as extra payments to pay off his home loan years faster. He walked on. A week or so prior to sending this book to print he called me and said he switched to a lower fixed rate of 2.19 per cent per annum and dropped his loan repayments down by a whopping $1500 a month. Not even his Professionals Package could offer that!

The bottom line is you need to get the right credit cards and loans for your own specific needs, otherwise you could end up paying for much more than you need.

Quick question – do you have the right credit card or home loan for you? If not, perhaps it's time to make a change. You can save plenty here and this will contribute to any surplus you may create (especially after you've gone through the process of reducing your expenses following some of the ideas I suggested in Chapter 4).

INTEREST RATE RISES – THE NATURAL BORN ENEMY OF YOUR DEBTS

Interest rates are clearly a very important element when it comes to debt as they essentially determine the price of the money you are borrowing. In other words, when interest rates go up, the price of money goes up; when rates fall, the price comes down.

Take, for instance, a rise in home loan rates by 0.5 per cent per annum (which is not out of the realms of possibility as we move out of the COVID-19 recovery actions). For a loan of $500,000 the monthly repayments would increase from $2,094 to $2,230 per month an increase of $136 per month. Not much, you might say, over the life of the loan. But ... and this is a big but ... it would add an extra $49,087 in interest to a brand new thirty-year, $500,000 loan. That's where the interest rate rise becomes the natural born enemy of debt.

The bottom line is you have to protect yourself as much as you can from rising interest rates. When the market is low, look to fix at least half or all of your loan so when rates rise again (and you can bet they will) you will be protected.

Different people have different strategies. One of my clients, for example, wanted the peace of mind of having her repayments fixed at the same level for the next five years so that she could get her budget under control. That's not everybody's cup of tea, but if it's a measure that will help you gain control of your expenses and break you out of the pay-to-pay cycle, then go for it.

In any event your best bet is to always talk to a mortgage expert first. When rates rise, credit cards and other forms of short-term loans are also generally affected, therefore, if you do see rates rise, look around for a credit card that suits your needs, with perhaps a lower rate.

GETTING YOUR DEBTS UNDER CONTROL

Here comes the fun stuff.

One of the biggest problems with keeping your debt under control is you often end up having a number of debt repayments that fall due at different times during the month. Plus, they all have different interest rates and different amounts you need to repay. This is a real hassle to manage, especially if you've got all of your other bills to pay in the meantime. No wonder so many people live from pay to pay as these uncoordinated debts can be incredibly debilitating.

To overcome this, and to get yourself on a path out of the pay-to-pay cycle, here are five options:

1. CONSOLIDATE YOUR DEBTS

Combine all your debts into one loan (be it a personal loan, or into your home loan if you've got one). The benefit of doing this is you will be able to get a lower interest rate (if you are combining credit card and store card debts into a personal loan or home loan, for example), plus you will only have one repayment, which can really help you synchronise your money flows between pay days. Let me give you an example to show you the power of this. A past client of mine had three credit cards with a total of $35,000 owing, and a home loan of $265,000, and was stuck in the pay-to-pay cycle, paying around $2700 per month. Essentially, she had four different dates and four different amounts she had to pay back.

Her mortgage repayment was around $1900 per month and she was shelling out about $600 a month on her credit cards but was barely covering the minimum repayments. The bottom line was she was not getting anywhere, and her credit cards were crippling her.

Luckily, she had enough equity in her home to be able to extend her home loan to $300,000. This then took her back to a thirty-year loan term. It was a strategy to go one step back in order to go ten steps forward!

"Uncoordinated payment of debts can be so debilitating ... no wonder people live pay to pay."

The repayments on her new combined loan were around $2000, $500 less than her previous home loan and credit card. The key to making this move successful however was to make extra payments to her home loan of about $400 per month, leaving her with $100 to spend on whatever she wanted.

If you don't have a home loan but have credit card debts that are out of control, a good idea may be to combine them into a low interest rate credit card with perhaps a zero percent balance transfer for six months or so. Please note, you will still have to make the base minimum repayments for that term and any new charges will be at the card's rate.

Alternatively, you may consider combining all your cards into one personal loan. This will give you fixed payments you can stick to. One thing to remember about this strategy is you need to first reduce the limit on your current credit card (so you don't get into trouble again). The key is now to also focus on paying the card off in full each month. Otherwise you'll find yourself right back in the debt cycle all over again.

If you've got store credit cards or a buy now, pay later arrangement, chances are you could be paying up to 27 per cent per annum interest if you break the contract or make a late payment. If you think you won't be able to make the payment exactly on time, get the heck out of them as fast as you can and consolidate them into a personal loan or your home loan. Whatever you do, shut down each of them after they are paid out and please try and resist the temptation of their enticing mailings. Just say no. You don't need them. The old Charles Dickens quote sums up these types of deals perfectly: "Credit is a system whereby a person who cannot pay gets another person who can pay to guarantee that he can pay." Think about that!

2. PAY YOUR DEBTS DOWN FASTER

If you've been doing your homework from Chapter 4 you might start to see some extra money being left over after all your expenses are paid. The trick with this extra money is to take some of it and make extra repayments. To show you what I mean, let's use the example of the client I mentioned a few seconds ago who combined her home loan and three credit cards. Remember I suggested she make extra monthly repayments of $400 on her new loan right from the word go, instead of the full $500 she was saving. The reason why I left it at $400 was to give her what I call "breathing space money" so she could enjoy her life a little.

At first she wasn't very keen to put the $400 a month onto the loan as extra payments as she wanted to have even more "breathing space money", but I convinced her by showing her how much she could save if she simply made an extra payment of $400 a month to her thirty-year loan at 2.91 per cent per annum. By paying the $400 she stood to save approximately $14,756 in interest, and chop two years and ten months off the life of the loan. Clearly, the greater the dollar value of extra repayments she made, the more she would save in time and interest. This is a great example of compound interest working in the favour of the borrower and not the lender. You can see that a great deal of interest is saved and not paid on the loan. When she saw these figures she literally jumped over the desk and kissed me. See what joy I bring to the world!

One thing I need to point out to you, as I did to my client, is all this assumes the interest rate stays the same and she keeps up her payments. We all know in the real world rates will change, but I don't think my client is going to reduce her payments any time soon after what she knows now.

If you want to know how this can apply to your loans, simply log onto <www.infochoice.com.au>, select Banking, then Home Loans, then Extra Repayments Calculator and give it a go.

3. KEEP ON GOING AS YOU ARE

Perhaps this is not the perfect solution as it doesn't actually get you anywhere. As I said before, if you have a credit card and keep paying just the minimum, it could take you up to twenty years or more to pay it off. Plus, if you keep on spending on that same card you'll pretty much never pay it off. A very bad financial situation to be in.

The same thing goes with your home loan. If you keep paying it off monthly and don't make any extra payments, you'll pretty much spend your life paying a lot of interest (this is when compound interest works in favour of the lender). Again, not a good strategy.

The bottom line is, **staying the same should not be an option**. If you are happy with that then I suggest you **close this book right now**. But don't go complaining in a few years, when you are about to retire, that you are poor and can't afford anything. Sure, these are harsh words, but sometimes they have to be said. You simply can't sit back and wait for the world to come to you.

4. DECLARE YOURSELF PERSONALLY INSOLVENT

I hope you never have to do this as it will have a massive impact on your short-term and long-term financial future. However, if you feel you are so close to the edge you might topple in, call a credit counsellor who can work with you to set up arrangements with the people you owe money to. Their services are free, and you can find them on Nastional Debt Helpline's website www.ndh.org.au (click on the link at the top to find a free credit counsellor near you). Don't put your head in the sand if you have a problem. Get help sooner rather than later, as your creditors will be nicer to you if you come to them earlier ... not ninety days after the bill is due!

Benjamin Franklin's great quote sums this up beautifully: "Creditors have better memories than debtors."

Personal Insolvency is not a very nice experience. I hope you will have the smarts to seek help before it's too late. I've seen too many people say they have too much pride to see a credit counsellor. But they are the unfortunate ones who end up being a personal insolvent statistic. Speaking of which, the number of people entering into personal insolvency in Australia is on the rise thanks to COVID-19, with a total of 12,000 personal insolvencies to May 2020. In fact, in the two-week period from March 23 2020 to April 5 2020, 1019 Australians applied for personal insolvency. Unfortunately, this figure will increase in the fallout of the impending financial tsunami caused by COVID19. So please, I repeat, please take as much from the tips in this book as you can and get your yourself prepared.

5. FOLLOW MY DEBT BUSTER PROGRAM

If you've got a couple of credit cards, perhaps a personal loan, a buy now, pay later deal and maybe even a home loan, this Debt Buster Program will literally show you a way of getting out of the debt doldrums quick smart. And, of course, out of the pay-to-pay cycle.

This program simply uses the principle of paying more, more often to debts that have the shortest time to pay off. (I'll explain more in a second.) It's also unique as it challenges the old theory of paying off your highest rate debt first, primarily as it is based around the size of the minimum repayment and how much you owe instead. It works particularly well for people with multiple debts such as credit cards, personal loans and home loans.

Before you start the program, check with your lender to see if you can make extra repayments. If you can't, the program won't work. While you are talking with your lenders, see if you can do some fancy footwork and reduce your payments somehow. (Ask for a reduction in your interest rate on your credit card, etc. It all makes a difference.) To make the program work properly you'll need to put in some serious effort and follow it religiously until all your debts are paid off. Yes, all the way through. This may be five years. Better than thirty or forty, huh? Trust me, it does work. Once you get started, I guarantee you'll get hooked as you watch your debts falling one by one with ever-increasing speed. There are no tricks. It's just a simple process that requires you to keep doing it over and again.

HERE'S HOW THE DEBT BUSTER PROGRAM WORKS

All you are doing in this program is ranking your debts in order of how long it will take to pay them off (assuming you are paying them back at minimum repayments).

Start by selecting the debt with the shortest time to pay and add a small amount of extra money. We'll call it "starter money" for now. (You'll see where you get this from in a moment.)

Add this extra amount to the minimum required repayment you are already making each month, and then continue this until that debt is paid off. (Of course, you are also keeping up your other minimum repayments on your other debts all the while.)

By paying extra on the debt that has got the shortest time to pay you'll logically end up paying it off even faster. This will have a great booster effect on you as it will prove to you that you can get rid of your debts without really changing your lifestyle too much. (Hint: Even though your minimum monthly repayment required will go down during this process, keep paying the same minimum repayment amount you first started on at the beginning of the program – this will speed things up even more.)

If you think that's good, wait until you hear this! After paying out your first debt you will now have some extra money (the minimum repayment amount for the first debt, plus the extra starter money you were paying each month). Instead of going out and spending it, the Debt Buster Program requires you to then select the debt that has the second shortest time to pay off.

Simply make your normal minimum repayments for the second debt but now add to it the total monies from the repayment money for the first debt, plus the extra payment you were making. Now you'll really pick up speed in paying back debt number two. Again, keep the exact amount of extra repayments all the way through and don't get complacent. Your debt-free life is just around the corner.

Now let's say debt one and debt two were credit cards and debt three is a home loan. Here, you simply add the starter money and extra monies left over from debt one and debt two to your regular repayments for your home loan, and you'll be eating into your home loan at a frenetic rate. Use any extra repayments calculator from <www.infochoice.com.au> to see how long it will take you to be totally debt free! You will be amazed.

THE MECHANICS OF THE DEBT BUSTER PROGRAM

The program sounds great, but how do you actually do it? Glad you asked. Just follow the four steps below:

STEP 1. FIND A BIT OF EXTRA MONEY TO ADD TO A PAYMENT (YOUR "STARTER MONEY")

A good way to start is to use what I call the ten per cent rule. Either take ten per cent of your income, if you can afford it, or ten per cent of your total debts (the total required monthly repayments for all your credit cards, personal loans and home loans) and use it to make an extra payment. You are probably saying, "Yeah, right, where do I get that from?" Well, hopefully you've done your homework from Chapter 4 and changed your spending habits so you should have some extra money to play with. Or you have invested in the 28 Day Budget Blitz to find extra cash.

The key here is you will need to have the amount you wish to allocate available all the way through the Debt Buster Program. If you haven't done so, go back to Chapter 4 and find some money.

Try for the ten per cent either way (of your income or your expense total), whichever is the lower of the two amounts. But please, please keep this starter money at the ready, otherwise the program won't work.

STEP 2. LIST ALL OF YOUR DEBTS

In the Debt Buster template list the type of loan, the latest amount outstanding and the minimum payment required.

STEP 3. WORK OUT THE BUSTER RATE

This is a simple ratio that will help you determine which debts you pay first under the Debt Buster Program. Essentially, the Buster Rate will give you the number of months it will take you to pay off a debt (assuming no additions are made to the debt amount). This is a very important bit of information, and it is critical to your success in the Debt Buster Program.

To calculate the Buster Rate, simply divide the amount of a debt by the minimum monthly payment required. Do this for all your debts: your credit cards, personal loans, store credit and your home loan if you've got one. Again, add this information into the Debt Buster template.

STEP 4. WORK OUT YOUR REPAYMENT PRIORITY

All you need to do here is look at the Buster Rate and rank your debts accordingly from the lowest to the highest Buster Rate score. In other words, if a debt has a Buster Rate of forty and another has a Buster Rate of twenty then the debt with the twenty is a higher priority. Remember this score represents the number of months it will take to pay back a loan, therefore the smaller number is the one that gets the highest priority. You can knock it off faster, hence giving you the confidence to knock off the rest, one by one.

In this column, simply use the numbers 1, 2, 3, 4 to rank the priority of your debts. Please note, if you end up with the same Buster Rate for two debts, always use the debt with the higher amount owing as a higher priority to pay off. This means you'll quickly get rid of much more debt.
The Debt Buster
I'm going to give you another template to follow, but this time I'm actually going to put an example in it to help when you are doing it on your own. By the way, log onto my website <www.budgetblitz.com.au> to download it.

Debt Name	Amount Outstanding $	Minimum monthly Repayment $	Buster Rate	Repayment Priority
Credit Card A	$4,000	$80	50	4
Credit Card B	$5,500	$110	50	3
Personal Loan	$10,000	$350	29	1
Store Card	$11,000	$300	37	2
Home Loan	$404,195*	$1,123	359	5
TOTAL	**$434,695**	**$3,425**	**525**	

* This was a home loan my client took out at $267,000. By the time you add interest to it of around $404,195 (over the 30-year term) the total ended up being $434,695. That's why lenders love you when you get a home loan over a longer period of time. And especially when you don't pay back early!

The figures in the template are actual examples from a client of mine who needed help desperately to get out of the debt cycle and, more importantly, the pay-to-pay cycle. When he came to meet me he was so far in debt he struggled to make all his payments and could hardly enjoy his life. As you can see, he was $434,695 in debt and faced a total of 525 months of debt. Obviously, that would come down over time as he paid his debts, however at that point in time there was a long road of debt ahead.

With a net after tax income of $4,250 per month he was barely scraping through. The first thing I did was to look at all his expenses, in a similar way to what I did for myself in Chapter 4.

Together we managed to find him an extra $450 a month. This $450 was the easy stuff. There was a whole lot more, but it would do for a start. Instead of using the ten per cent rule as I mentioned in the Debt Buster Program, I allocated $400 (a little bit less than ten per cent of his net monthly income) to use it as his Starter Money. The $50 difference was going to be, as I call it, his "breathing space money". Not much, I know, but better than nothing (that's perhaps a takeaway meal a week). Look, life's too short and you have to have some little luxuries.

Now I could have suggested he consolidate his debts into his home loan but, because the value of his house had fallen, he now had a loan-to-value ratio (how much you owe divided by how much your property is worth) of 85 per cent which meant he would now have to pay Lenders Mortgage insurance – an extra expense of a few thousand dollars he couldn't afford. So instead of consolidating we went for the option of paying back more by using the Debt Buster Program.

"Instead of paying debt for forty-four years, he can clear it in nine years using the Debt Buster Program."

With the extra $400 as our Starter Money we then started on the debt with the number one priority. In this case it was the personal loan. Luckily, my client could make extra payments on this. (By the way, not all personal loans allow you to, so check first.) We simply added the $400 to the $350 he was currently paying, making a new total of $750 per payment. At that rate he would pay his first debt back in thirteen months. That's a saving of fifteen months. Not bad, considering that he was originally looking at twenty-nine months.

After the thirteen months of repayments, while also keeping up with all his other payments, it was time to get to his next debt. This was the Store Card, where he paid a minimum payment of $300 a month. Now you'll start to see the Debt Buster Program come into its own.

With the $750 that was now available after paying off the first debt, we added this to the minimum repayment for the Store Card debt, which gave us a new monthly payment of $1050.

All we had to do now was pay the $1050 per month on the amount of $11,000. (Note that this amount was probably less given that the minimum amounts for this debt were paid for the thirteen months. For this example, I assumed that the amount had stayed the same.)

After paying the $1050 per month, this Store Card debt was easily paid back in only ten and a half months. That's twenty months earlier than if he would have paid it back with the minimum amounts. See the power of the Debt Buster Program?

Then came the Credit Card B debt (priority number three). Here the minimum payments were $110 per month. But once we added the $1050 per month left over from paying out the Personal Loan and Store Card debt, he was able to pay a total of $1160 toward the Credit Card B debt. By making payments at that rate the debt of $5500 was paid in only 4.7 months. That's a saving of 45.3 months off the original debt!

Credit card A (the fourth debt in order of priority) was then a cakewalk. With an accelerated repayment of $1240 ($1160 plus the minimum repayment of $80) this debt of $4000 was wiped out in only 3.2 months.

Okay, let's take a breather and recap for a moment.

Before we started my client was facing 13.8 years of paying back his short-term debts (debts with priority one through to four) at minimum monthly payments. After following the Debt Buster Program, he did it in 31.5 months ... that's only 2.6 years.

Impressed?

Well, you should be.

Can you do it? *You bet.*

Is it hard? *Nope.*

All this sounds good, but you haven't seen anything yet. Remember, under the template I mentioned he also had a home loan of $267,000 but was faced with paying back close to $404,195 (including interest over his thirty-year loan at 2.91 per cent per annum).

Well, things are changing. He has just started to make additional payments to his loan after about five years into it.

Paying an extra $1,240 per month (or $620 a fortnight – don't forget you save a whole lot more if you pay weekly or fortnightly) he is going to save approximately $61,777 in interest and carve fifteen years and four months off his loan.

Therefore, by using the Debt Buster Program he will be short-term debt free in just over two years and own his own home outright in just on ten years (assuming he consistently keeps up the extra payments of $1240).

Not bad, considering that before he met me he was staring down the barrel of about forty-five years paying off debts and living from pay to pay (just to scrape up enough money to pay his debts).

He is so focused now that every extra dollar he gets he uses to make extra payments.

Voilà!

The incredible power of the Debt Buster Program!

ORGANISING YOUR DEBTS

One last thing I need to talk about before we move on to the next chapter is that to make the Debt Buster Program work even smoother, I recommend you set up auto deductions for the payment of your debts (if you haven't already done so). That way, you'll ensure your payments are made on time so you don't incur any unnecessary interest bills.

Speaking of interest bills, lenders do from time to time make errors with loans (particularly around the calculation of interest) therefore you can either check each statement when you get it or buy a software programme called Mortgage Watch Dog. Check it out at <www.mortgagewatchdog.com.au>.

IT TAKES GUTS AND TIME

Pretty much all of the stuff I've been talking about in this chapter requires you to put in some serious effort both in terms of personal sacrifice and time.

The process may look daunting at the start, but always remember when your back is against the wall you only have one way to go.

How did you think my client felt when I showed him he had a mere 525 months to go to pay off all his loans at the rate he was going?

Not good, I can assure you.

But he persevered, and is now well on his way to being debt free in a fraction of that time.

You may or may not be in a similar situation to my client, but either way I hope you have taken some real tips out of this chapter (especially my mum's tips on debt) which will help you recognise the problem early and take control of your debts.

It's about not only getting out of the debt cycle, but also out of the dreaded pay-to-pay cycle.

Let's face it, once you get rid of the debts you will have money to invest. Won't that be a lovely feeling?

CHAPTER 6
SETTING A COURSE FOR YOUR FINANCIAL FREEDOM

Thanks to the magic of the last two chapters, your finances should now be starting to take shape and hopefully showing signs of returning to the black. If this is the case, then you are well on your way to breaking out of the pay-to-pay cycle.

Of course, as I've said many times in this book, the changes you are putting into place will take a while to happen. But if you are showing signs of being in the black it augurs well for the future.

Speaking of the future, now you've got some extra cash rolling in, you are going to dust off those old savings skills so you can properly tap into the extra cash and build up some – dare I say the word – savings.

I know this may be a word you haven't used in a while, but it's my challenge to reacquaint you with the fine art of saving and wealth accumulation.

To start you off I'm going to share with you a few old-fashioned but effective savings techniques. And then I'll show you how to build up an Emergency Savings Fund (the just-in-case money), plus

I'll give you a few pointers on how you can use your extra money to develop a set of passive income streams that will ultimately give you the freedom to one day say goodbye to your boss (in the nicest possible way, of course!).

At this point you may be thinking, well that's sounds all fine and dandy, but I have always been a hopeless saver and I just don't think that a single chapter in a book is going to change me. I can understand that, but let me assure you that what you're about to read is pretty simple stuff and all you have to do is to pick whichever basic method (or methods) you think may work for you and give it a try.

THE MONEY ALLOWABLE – THE BASIC EQUATION FOR SAVINGS AND WEALTH

Before I speak about some of the techniques of saving, I want to have a quick chat about the Money Allowable concept I introduced you to in Chapter 1.

If you recall, savings were put on the expenses side of the equation (Income – Savings – Expenses = Money Allowable) I believe the real art of saving is to pay yourself, **no matter what**. Even if you only save $2 a pay you're actually breaking through a tough psychological barrier and proving to yourself that you are capable of saving. Sure, it's not much. But like so many things with money it's all about a mindset.

I know I've been focusing a lot in this book about mindsets and money personalities, but eighty per cent of your money woes are in your head. All you have to do is understand them and confront them and you're almost there.

On the other side of the equation is the amount of money left over after your savings and expenses are deducted from your total income. This is the Money Allowable amount that will either be a positive or negative figure. Clearly, your main aim with the Money

Allowable amount is to turn it from a negative amount to a positive one as you transition out of to the pay-to-pay cycle. To do this, you may either need to increase your income or reduce your expenses even further. Please note that at no stage should you ever reduce the amount of savings just to give you a positive Money Allowable. Your savings must be held sacred, however small. Always keep the notion of "pay yourself first" in your head.

When you end up with a positive Money Allowable on an ongoing basis, you will be able to allocate this to your wealth creation money (I'll talk about that later). That's why I've called it the Money Allowable as it allows you to choose what you do with your money.

HOW TO REGAIN THE LOST ART OF SAVING

In October 2019, Compare the Market released a Financial Consciousness Index (FCI) which showed just 56 per cent of Australians save at least 10 per cent of their income In that very same report, it revealed that 13.4 million Australians don't have emergency savings to fall back on if they are unable to earn an income for more than three months. The really scary thing about this is, this report was released in October, and Australia literally shut down from February to June 2020 as a result of COVID-19, forcing millions out of work.

Worse still, the report mentioned that 7.3 million Australians would rely totally on the Government and 4.3 million would have to rely on family and friends for support to continue to pay their bills and mortgages.

Thanks to JobKeeper and the JobSeeker bonus, the multi-billion dollar COVID-19 bailouts by the Australian government, and the mortgage deferral programs provided by banks, the impact of COVID-19 has been reduced. For now.

Remember I keep mentioning the financial tsunami? Well the first wave will hit Australia when the JobSeeker bonus and JobKeeper are phased out. As a result of this millions more people will lose their jobs. Hence, more people will be forced to sell their home and more people will be kicked out of their rental accommodation as the funds dry up. The second tsunami, and possibly a bigger one, will come when global companies start to contract and withdraw staff from Australia and close Australian based subsidiaries, and investment and the demand for Australian exports drop.

Do we have a bleak future for the next few years? Yes.

The financial fallout from COVID-19 is without doubt one of the biggest financial crises we have seen to date and it is the mother of Money Monsters.

I apologise if I'm starting to sound a tad depressing, but we all need to stop and take stock of the overall economic world around us and how it impacts on our daily lives. That's why you need to build up a buffer zone of savings or Emergency Money as soon as possible so that you have a pot of cash set aside to ride out the downturn when it comes.

The art of saving is quite simple and relatively painless. Nowadays you can do this on "autopilot" by simply setting up automatic deductions from your salary or from your existing bank accounts, or setting up a round up account and channelling whatever amount you wish to regularly save into a high interest, at call savings account. Because it all happens automatically you don't see it; by not seeing it, you won't miss it. Simple, really. You'll even be pleasantly surprised after some time as the amount builds up (especially if you don't touch it).

I've been doing my own autopilot type of saving over the years to prove that it can easily be done. I have $50 taken out of my transaction account (which doesn't earn me any interest) each pay and put into a high interest savings account and I've saved close to $14,000 (before tax) in five years. Not bad, huh? That's my emergency money.

Incredibly, the trick to saving is that there is no trick. All you need is to do is follow a particular method and keep on doing it. That's it.

Speaking of methods, here's a few of my favourites that may be of some interest to you. Have a read and pick one you relate to and give it a go. Once you start, I guarantee you'll use a few, if not all, of the four methods.

1. THE PERCENTAGE METHOD

Calculate five or 10 per cent of your after-tax salary and ask your pay officer to automatically deposit that amount each week into a high interest savings account. Start with a small amount each pay at first until you get comfortable with this concept then increase it each year. Most banks and specialist deposit-taking institutions offer high interest accounts, so sign yourself up. To find the institutions that offer high interest accounts visit <www.ratecity.com.au>. You can find and compare high interest savings accounts that will best suit you.

2. THE $5 NOTE METHOD

I love this one. Every time you get a five dollar note keep it in your purse/wallet and, at the end of the month, deposit your stash into your high interest savings account. If $5 is too much, try just about any denomination.

3. THE ROUNDING METHOD

This one I call the "silent winner". All you need to do is round off your salary to the nearest zero and save whatever the amount you round off. In other words, if you earn say $420 a week take the $20 and put it in your high interest savings account. Again, put this on autopilot so you don't miss the money going out.

4. THE PAY RISE METHOD

If you are fortunate enough to get a pay rise (especially during COVID-19), think about putting a fair amount of that into your savings. You didn't have this money before, so it's a perfect way to start a savings program. If you have debts I suggest you follow my 40/40/20 rule: put 40 per cent to your debts, 40 per cent to savings and 20 per cent to fun (I've been pretty nice by giving you 20 per cent). Of course, you can adjust these amounts as you see fit, but it may be a good place to start.

5. THE TAP AND GO METHOD

This method works by transferring money into your savings account every time you use your debit card and tap and go. With COVID-19 cash and coins have been put aside, so maybe now is a good time to get digital and set up a round up savings account. These accounts are brilliant as they help you save without you knowing you're saving. Essentially, they round up the amount you spend to the nearest dollar (or whatever limit you set) and transfer it directly into your saving account. For example, say you buy something worth $20 with your tap and go debit card, immediately $1 extra (or whatever amount you set) will be transferred to your round up savings account. It's that simple. It's that invisible. So, every time you tap and go, you are not only spending, you are saving. It really adds up!

SAVINGS AIN'T SAVINGS

If you were like me, you probably grew up with your first introduction to the concept of savings being a piggy bank or passbook, which you put some money into and gave to the teacher when the person from the bank came around.

Unfortunately, this type of savings approach is pretty much one-dimensional, and only teaches you how to save money in a single location and then spend it. Think back to the number of times you raided your poor old piggy bank when you were a kid. Back then all you had was one place where you had all of your savings, and you probably raided it, usually to the detriment of longer-term savings goals.

What you need is a multidimensional approach to the concept of saving so that you can start allocating your money into separate accounts that represent the different areas of your life. Instead of one big savings account from which you do everything (like the old piggy bank when you were a kid), you need to set up a number of separate accounts to manage your savings properly. This way you can set individual savings goals for each category and ensure you save something and not end up with this one big account you constantly dip in and out of.

This multidimensional approach will also help you to make a clear distinction between your spending money and your saving money. For your spending money (money for bills, entertainment, food, etc) you need to set up a separate low fee transaction account and again have your pay officer put in what you need.

If they can't do that, you'll have to allocate your pay by yourself into your different accounts. That's why having a good handle on how much you spend comes in handy – you can, with a degree of certainty, allocate money appropriately between your savings, debts and spending.

"The multi-dimensional approach will help you distinguish between spending and saving."

For your saving money (which, by the way, is a combination of the S and the MA from the Money Allowable equation) you can now set up your different savings accounts. I prefer five high interest savings accounts that are set up on autopilot. All have regular amounts put into them each pay day. This way I can budget my savings, so to speak.

I have a formula I use to allocate my savings money into these separate accounts, however it does change from time to time to reflect my situation. Just like the 40/40/20 rule I mentioned a few seconds ago, I follow a little more elaborate 10/30/10/30/20 rule. In other words, from the total of my savings money (the S and the MA from the money allowable) I allocate per pay day 10 per cent to my emergency money fund, 30 per cent to paying down debts, 10 per cent for my short-term purchases, 30 per cent for long-term purchases and 20 per cent for my investments.

With that in mind, here's those five different types of savings accounts I mentioned above, together with a brief explanation of each. As you'll see they are pretty easy to follow and will more than likely help you set up some sort of structure to your savings.

As you read them, have a think about how you can put some – if not all – into action yourself.

1. EMERGENCY SAVINGS FUND ACCOUNT

In the opening of this chapter, I mentioned the Compare the Market Survey where 13.4 million Australians admitted they did not have enough emergency money to last beyond three months if a disaster struck. Remember, also the concept of Money Monsters. Well, COVID-19 was certainly the mother of all Money Monsters. Like any Money Monster, it couldn't be predicted, so all you could do was prepare for its eventuality. Your aim for emergency money therefore should be to save up to six months minimum of your total expenses. Make that your objective and follow any of the savings techniques or those in the 28 Day Budget Blitz to reach it.

2. DEBT SAVINGS ACCOUNT

If you've got a major debt like a home loan it is definitely worth your while to set up a mortgage offset account to hold your Debt Savings. Essentially, every bit of money you save in this account gets applied to your loan at the end of the month and reduces the amount of interest you pay overall. In other words, your interest bill for your loan is calculated using an offset account by subtracting the balance outstanding on the loan less the amount in your offset savings account. Therefore, the more money you have in this account (and left untouched, mind you) the less interest you'll pay and the faster you'll pay off your home loan.

If you don't have a home loan account, and perhaps only a credit card, the Debt Saving Account may help you save up money each month to either pay off your credit card in full, or to use as the extra payment money we spoke about in the Debt Buster Program. If you don't have any debts you clearly won't need this account. Therefore, whatever money you were going to put in there, redirect it to your Investment Account. This will grow your assets at a greater pace.

3. SHORT-TERM PURCHASES ACCOUNT

Here's something different. Instead of going straight out and buying something, why not start saving for it? Interesting concept, I know, given the "got to have it now" society we live in. But why not save up for something? Try it, you may like it. In fact, if you've got kids see if you can instil this idea in them early on. Otherwise you'll be forever putting your hands in your pocket buying them the latest and greatest thing, which is clearly sending the wrong message. This type of savings account may not be for everyone, but it is nevertheless a great way to teach you how to save up for things you want. You never know, half-way through your saving you may discover you really don't want it after all. Much better than going out and buying it on credit and being stuck with it!

4. LONG-TERM PURCHASES ACCOUNT

If you are looking to save up for a house, car, boat or anything that requires a big deposit or a lot of cash, then this is the account for you. You'll have to nominate a greater percentage of your savings allocation for this account (in my case I put 30 per cent in here as I'm saving up for my next home) in order to save up the amount quickly. One thing you need to know about this account: to get to your savings goal quickly, you need to keep this account clean. By that I mean, it's got to be a separate, standalone account you never dip into.

5. INVESTING ACCOUNT

One way to save and invest at the same time that is worth investigating is a rounding up savings account called Raiz. This account collects your spare change from your tap and go purchases (you set a limit of the round up) and they help you select an exchange traded fund to invest in. Not a bad way to invest your small change, and it can really grow over time. Check them out at <www.raizinvest.com.au>.

As you can see, there are many different ways to invest; it all depends on how much you have, your tolerance to risk and what your ultimate goal is.

When I had my financial planning practice, I had a lot of people coming to me and saying, "I just want to be rich". When I asked them what they meant by that (How rich? By when? What do you have to start? What sort of risk do you want to take?) they get this look of horror on their face as they expect me to have all the answers. Remember, financial advisers only have the answers when you provide answers to their questions. In that way, you can both develop a solid plan to provide you with both capital growth and income growth.

"Money professionals only have the answers when you provide some answers of your own."

Now, before you go and say "Wait a minute, aren't I going to be slugged with heaps of fees here, and all my hard-earned savings will be eaten up?" It all depends on how you set them up. If your pay officer at work will allow you to nominate multiple accounts, you can easily do this without incurring any extra fees. Just tell them the amounts. If you can't do that, have your pay put into a low fee or no fee account and set up your own auto transfers. Be careful here: you need to keep well within your number of free transactions, otherwise you'll end up paying too much in excess fee charges. A number of banks offer multiple splits to their transaction accounts, so I'd recommend you log onto <www.ratecity.com.au> to compare fee-free high interest accounts and transaction accounts.

FINANCIAL FREEDOM – THE NEXT STEP

When I was writing this part, I asked a number of my friends and colleagues to describe for me what they thought financial freedom meant to them.

As to be expected, I got a range of answers: never having to work for a boss again; being filthy rich; having just enough money to live a normal life without going to work for someone; having enough money to determine where I go, what I do and who I see each day. Almost all of them were adamant they didn't want to work for a boss or keep to specific hours each day, five days a week. They all wanted the ability to go to the beach, sleep in when they wanted and go on holidays without filling in millions of forms and kissing the feet of their boss to get some time off.

For me, financial freedom means having enough cash flow and assets to have choice in my life.

Instead of working in the corporate world, I've chosen to work for myself, which enables me to work when I want to work, earn when I want to earn and sleep in whenever I want to (my personal favourite).

Clearly, running your own business has its own set of challenges (given my experiences of a few years back), but nevertheless I enjoy the freedom of building my own ventures. Notice the word ventures? I'm not trying to show off here, but what I'm trying to tell you is you need to develop a series of income streams, not just one. (More on that in a second.) Ultimately, I'll sell my businesses, or parts thereof, and receive an ongoing royalty (or take the cash and got to the next thing) which will give me a whole new set of choices.

My dad did this back in the 1980s when he sold the three courier businesses he had operated across Sydney since 1960. These companies provided him with a very good income stream over the years, which allowed him to buy other assets. With this income and the proceeds of the sales of his companies, he built up a significant investment portfolio from which he now receives a very good return in his retirement.

I said retirement, but it was Mum who wouldn't let him work anymore. He says he could keep going until he's a hundred, and he probably could. He could have stopped work many years earlier, as he had sufficient assets and passive income flows to give him enough cash to do whatever he and Mum wanted. But once an entrepreneur, always an entrepreneur.

Dad's a man who came from nothing and started up his own business after many years working for someone else. He didn't like "working for the man" but knew he had to build up enough cash to start his business and take that "leap of faith". Well, like any business in its early years, he did pretty much everything in his company. He was the salesperson, the bookkeeper and even the courier driver (this was a courier company!). In fact, he was so overloaded with work but so cash-strapped (don't forget he had a wife and three hungry boys to feed) he had to do a U-turn on the Sydney Harbour

Bridge one day just to go back and pick up another job so that he could deliver two jobs in the city at the same time. He put his heart and soul into the business, plus a lot of blood, sweat and tears. In fact, he even risked his own life many times during all the petrol strikes in the '70s, carting barrels of petrol (yes, petrol) in the back of his station wagon so his drivers could have enough petrol to do the deliveries. Sure, it was hard for him (and very risky) but it goes to show that anyone can do it. He didn't even have a degree.

The lessons I learned from Dad – and you can also learn – is to be happy with what you do, be prepared to put in some effort, manage the dividends you receive from it wisely and create an ongoing passive income stream so that you can do what you want to do.

ARE YOU READY FOR FINANCIAL FREEDOM?

Okay, now the $64 million question. Are you ready to be financially free? Ah! Before you answer that, I need you to take a close look at what your net worth by taking a quick snapshot of your assets and liabilities.

By simply listing all your assets (your savings, home, car, furniture, etc) and your liabilities (your home loan, personal loan and credit card debts), then totalling their values and subtracting your total liabilities from your total assets, you'll end up with your **net personal wealth**. This figure will show you quite simply how much you own, as opposed to how much you owe. A vital piece of knowledge to be able to adjust whatever you have to in order to ensure your financial future looks bright. (I'll show you want I mean in a minute.)

Putting this list together is fairly straightforward. (If you've ever applied for a loan you'll remember how easy it is.) Except here I've included a few extra categories so that we can analyse it better later. All of this won't take you very long if you use the template below or hop onto my website <www.budgetblitz.com.au> and download it. Most of the information you need should be easily available from the Cash FlowBudget Planner template you did in Chapter 3.

The only difficult things are the estimates of the value of your assets. For example, your home. The best way to value it correctly is to have a professional valuer come by, but that's going to extremes. You could have a real estate agent give you a figure, but they'll tell you a selling price. We all know the difference between a selling price and a buying price.

The quickest and cheapest way to get an estimate of the value of your home is to see what other houses in your area (with similar in features to yours) have sold for in the recent months. You can get this information from real estate agents or websites such as <www.corelogic.com.au>. Cars are very simple – go to online car sites such as <www.carsales.com.au>.

But when it comes to things like jewellery and furniture, things get a little cloudy and, dare I say it, emotional. With something like furniture we tend to think it's valued at much more than it's really worth, primarily because we inflate it for our insurance purposes. Try and sell it for what you bought it for. Even better, try and sell it in a hurry and see what price you end up getting.

Likewise, you need to be careful when you are placing a value on your jewellery. You think the ring your dead aunt gave you is worth a fortune? Perhaps not as much as you think. I know this all too well from when I tried to sell the engagement ring my fiancée gave back to me after she left. (One nice gesture at least.) As I wanted to get it out of my sight, and fast, I took it straight back to the place I bought it from. I've got to say, I was a tad disappointed (the understatement of the year!) when the jeweller offered to buy it back from me at half the price I'd paid only a few months earlier! Crikey, someone tell me the real value of engagement rings please.

Even though I was very upset, I didn't let my emotions get the better of me. Instead of accepting the first price I was offered, I held myself together and did a deal. Bottom line, I negotiated with the jeweller to take the ring on consignment (in other words, he would act as my sales agent and sell it in his shop for a price that I'd set). If he got the sale, I'd give him a commission.

Luckily he was a nice bloke (maybe he felt sorry for me, or could see he was getting two bites of the cherry) and accepted this. A few months later he sold it for the price I wanted (which, by the way, was $1000 over the price I originally paid). From that extra $1000 I gave him $800 for his troubles and off I went with the cash.

What did I do with the cash, you may be wondering? I invested it in a few stocks and they are now worth close on double the value of the original ring. Touché, ex-fiancée.

The moral of the above is not to get back at your ex, but to be conservative in the valuation of your assets. Otherwise you are just kidding yourself. I guess I was lucky with the ring, but as my mum always used to say "Sometimes good things come from bad things".

YOUR WEALTH SCORECARD

In the business world the wealth scorecard is called a Balance Sheet. It includes things like depreciation and retained earnings and all the other boring accounting things that will mean absolutely nothing to many of you, so I'll keep it simple.

First, here's a few tips on how to categorise your assets and liabilities:

Let's start with your assets. They are split into what's called current assets (things like your savings accounts that you can convert into cash right now) and non-current assets, like your house, your car, furniture and jewellery that I've just talked about. The reason why these are considered non-current is it will take you days, if not months, to sell them and turn them into cash.

When it comes to valuing your jewellery and furniture, remember what I said before – be ultra-conservative. Start with say 40 per cent of the value you have listed on your insurance policy and always think what you could get if you tried to sell them tomorrow on eBay or at a garage sale. That's the value you should use.

Finally, total them all up to reveal your Total Assets figure.

For your liabilities, start with your current debts, that is those that fall due in the short-term like your credit card, personal loan and store credit, and input the totals of their current outstanding amounts. Then, for your non-current liabilities (your home loan or investment loan) include your latest debt outstanding. Total up the current and non-current liabilities to reveal your Total Liabilities. Finally, subtract your Total Liabilities from your Total Debt to reveal your Net Asset Position.

YOUR WEALTH SCORECARD

Category	$
Assets	
Current Assets	
Your money in all your transaction accounts	
Your money in all your savings accounts	
Subtotal	
NON-CURRENT assets	
The market value of your home	
The market value of your car	
The market value of your furniture	
The market value of your jewellery	
The market value of your antiques	
Subtotal	
TOTAL ASSETS	
Liabilities	
Current Liabilities	
The total debt outstanding on your credit cards	
The total debt outstanding on your personal loan	
The total debt outstanding on your store credit	
The total debt outstanding on other loans	
Subtotal	
NON-CURRENT Liabilities	
The total debt outstanding on your home loan	
The total debt outstanding on your investment loan	
Subtotal	
TOTAL LIABILITIES	
TOTAL NET ASSETS (TOTAL ASSETS MINUS TOTAL LIABILITIES)	

CHAPTER 6

WHAT DOES YOUR STATEMENT OF ASSETS AND LIABILITIES TELL YOU AND WHAT CAN YOU DO TO IMPROVE YOUR SITUATION?

Not only will this statement tell you what your net asset position is (I'll come back to that in a second), it will also give you a few indicators of how well you are going in certain areas of your wealth creation. For instance, now you know the subtotals on your Current Assets and Current Liabilities, you can work out what I call your "Convert to Cash" ratio, which is simply a measure of your total current assets divided by your total current liabilities. It's a pretty simple calculation (Convert to Cash Ratio = Current Assets / Current Liabilities) and one that will tell you very quickly if you have to take some drastic measures to improve your cash flow.

For example, let's say your total current assets are $10,000 and your total current liabilities are $15,000. This gives you a ratio of only 0.66. In this instance, clearly you have more short-term debt than savings. Hence your road to financial freedom is somewhat blocked until you get this figure to at least a factor of 2. In other words, you need about two times the amount of current assets in order to be able to sell them and pay off your current liabilities and still not fall into a financial hole. To fix your situation, you will probably need to refer to the Debt Buster Program mentioned in Chapter 5.

Another ratio that comes out of your assets and liabilities figures is what's called the **Leverage Ratio**. This is especially relevant for those with mortgages. That is the amount of money you have borrowed as a percentage of your assets. To calculate it you simply need to divide Your Loan (for your home or investment) by your total assets.

This ratio comes in handy for two reasons. First, when you are going for a loan your lender uses it to determine the Loan to Valuation Ratio, that is the magic 80 per cent. Second, it gives you a very good reading as to how much real asset ownership you actually have. Let's face it, if you are highly leveraged because you have borrowed up to 90–100 per cent of the value of your home, you really don't own much of it and pretty much have no options other than pay it back as fast as you can. If, on the other hand, the ratio is low (which means you own more than you owe on your home) then, if you want, you can start to engage in some investment activities using that "equity" or ownership in your home.

In this situation you can borrow money to invest in an investment property or managed fund. To do this you need a stable income stream (to meet the extra repayments because you would be borrowing more), plus you'd definitely need to be comfortable with the extra risk of borrowing and investing. The wealth creation benefits of doing something like this are immense, as not only will you create potential tax savings (you can take advantage of negative gearing and tax deferred investments), you'll also be able to pay off your home debt faster (as you channel all the investment returns into your home loan first). Plus, you'll end up owning an extra investment that will not only provide you with capital growth but also an ongoing passive income stream.

Before I go on, let me give you a real-life example of this to show you how just about anyone can do it.

When I was a planner, a client of mine came to me and said she wanted to own "some sort of investment" in the next five years. Knowing she had a home with some equity in it, I suggested she borrow an extra $50,000 to invest in a diversified property fund that invested in commercial property, just as a start. Other than the good performance of this fund (although past performance should never be a total guide) this fund offered tax benefits where the tax on her investment returns were deferred until the time she sold the investment. By taking on the extra $50,000, her total twenty-five year home loan was now $160,000. Sure this was increasing her overall debt, but the new debt was good debt as it could be used to not only generate tax advantages but also to generate income that could go toward paying down the home loan, or bad debt. By borrowing an extra $50,000 for investment purposes, her repayments increased by $255 per month. However, the interest received from the investment was approximately $375 per month (tax deferred) putting her $120 ahead each month.

She was already paying $500 a month over her required repayments thanks to the Debt Buster Program, she then chose to pay $1,875 per month. The best part about this is, by making the extra payments she would now save approximately $113,000 in interest and pay her loan off fifteen years and three months earlier. This meant she would now own her home plus have a $50,000 investment portfolio in just under ten years.

Sure, this was only $50,000, but it's a great start. She is now talking about doing a lot more. (Please note that a strategy like this is very individual, so your best bet is to have a chat to a financial planner to investigate it more.)

The fourth ratio from your assets and liabilities figures is what's called the Debt to Assets Ratio. Effectively it calculates how much debt you have relative to your total assets. Unlike the leverage ratio, this looks at all your liabilities and all your assets. The calculation is therefore quite simple: divide your total liabilities by your total assets (Debt to Assets Ratio = Total liabilities / Total Assets). If you have a greater number of assets than liabilities (your ratio is greater than one) things are looking okay. However, if your ratio is less than one, things may have to change my friend.

Let's face it, if your assets fall in value, there's not much you can do except wait for the market to rise. But if your debts seem to be rising, you can certainly restructure them and make a number of changes (check out Chapter 5 for more).

The final measure is another way of seeing the debt to assets ratio, however it is simply a straight calculation of two total figures (your total assets minus your total liabilities). This is basically your Net Asset Position, and for your sake I truly hope it is in positive territory. That way you can use the equity you have in your assets to leverage investments to create a passive income stream, as I mentioned above.

If it's not positive, you may have to take some corrective action pretty fast, as I said before. Let's face it, debts somehow have a way of growing faster than assets, especially when you are in a negative asset position. Some of the actions you may need to take include a full debt restructure, a complete sell out and repayment of debts or a selling down of assets and downsizing of your loans and possibly your home.

With COVID-19, you may have to face this reality. (Check with your lender first to see what they can offer.) This one is a real hard pill to swallow I know, but always remember to go forward sometimes you need to go back a step.

I hope you can now see how important an assets and liabilities snapshot is when it comes to managing your future financial freedom. Without it (and your cash flow statement) you are literally flying blind. It may be boring, but as I keep on saying, this is your life and it's your money you're playing with.

Spend more time on it and you will have more to spend.

YOUR FIVE STEPS TO FINANCIAL FREEDOM

Okay, you've learned how to save again, how to get a snapshot of your net financial position and of course how to improve. Now let me show you how to set your own course for financial freedom. As I said before, one person's definition of financial freedom is different from another's, but nevertheless let me share with you what I consider to be the five key steps to gain financial freedom.

1. GET THE BASICS RIGHT

Throughout this book I've been showing you how to get out of the pay-to-pay cycle by giving you basic mechanical tasks. I've used them and I still use them. Yes, they've been tough to do. Yes, they've involved a lot of templates and numbers. But to get me out of the vicious cycle I had to do what I had to do. Knowing the basics and then following the procedures that someone has very carefully worked out and successfully implemented is the key. It does take time, so don't become a monk and live a pauper life in the meantime. Enjoy yourself while you get out of the cycle, but in moderation. And remember, you simply can't put your head in the sand and hope it all goes away. If I'd done that I'm sure I would have gone bankrupt (which is not a nice place to be). As I keep saying, there's no rocket science behind these basics and there's definitely no reason to try and overcomplicate things. Sure, things in the money world may sound complicated, but all you need to do is spend a little time improving your knowledge. Reading books and attending seminars are great ways to learn, but you need to read and attend the right ones. There's no point in reading a book or going to a seminar that tells you how to become a millionaire in seven easy steps if you don't have two dollars to rub together. You simply can't go straight from A to Z; you need to go one step at a time, especially if you are in the pay-to-pay cycle. Never forget, however, once you are out you still need to keep applying the basics as they are your foundation stone. Make them solid and your financial future will be solid.

2. HAVE THE RIGHT MINDSET

Ever heard the saying "You are what you say you are"? Well if you think you are hopeless with money then you will be, and you'll stay in the pay-to-pay cycle. However, if you believe in yourself and you've got the motivation to break out, then you will. If you also believe that once you break out you will be well on your way to financial freedom, chances are it will happen. You just have to get your head into a positive mode. I know that this may seem incredibly hard at times, but I for one have experienced some black times, especially when I was being rushed to hospital for the fourth time, the time I was told I might not see out of my left eye ever again and when my accountant made the call. Even though all these things happened to me in quick succession, I never gave up. I never will give up. Perhaps that's something you want to take from here and think twice about. Let's face it, there will always be someone somewhere worse off than you. My formula for being happy, and I know this is not a traditional thing to say in a money book, I laugh a lot.

The world is serious. COVID-19 reminded us of that. But COVID-19 also taught us how to focus on family and be closer to loved ones (via Zoom), but also to try and have a laugh. Don't be certifiable, but try to bring a little lightness to each of your situations. Life's too short to be gloomy.

While I'm on secrets here, you may be wondering if there is a particular mindset for being financially free? Yes, there is. You must constantly reassure yourself that nothing is impossible. A financially free person always finds ways to get what they want, and is not confined by what others say or tell them to do. Plus, they are not constrained by linear thoughts. They are positive, happy and above all empathetic to the needs of others. Give it a try and see how different your life becomes. Think positive and positive things will happen.

3. DEVELOP PASSIVE INCOME STREAMS

There are several ways to earn passive income, all of which require some effort to set up. So don't be fooled by the name passive! Planned and implemented properly, your activity will slow down but your ongoing income stream will keep increasing.

First, you can use your assets, as I mentioned a little earlier, to leverage investments. Depending on the level of risk you want to take, your cash flow and how much you have in assets to leverage, you can invest in managed funds, superannuation, tax deferred funds, the share market, investment property, fixed interest, antiques, and so on. All of which will generate appropriate capital and income returns that will provide you with a solid income stream. You will need professional assistance to set them up properly to provide you with a revenue stream, but as I always say, build a "Money Team". In other words, see if you can get to know a stockbroker, a mortgage broker, a financial planner and a tax accountant. If you've got no idea where to start, just ask your friends or family. Don't be afraid to call these professionals even if you don't have any money. If they're smart, they will realise you are on your way to financial freedom and should feel privileged to be invited to your team.

Second, you can start our own company or set up a business online. Many people see this as a very big part of their financial freedom, as by being their own boss they can call the shots and create something that will provide enough cash to build assets and ultimately a passive income. The sheer fact of being in their own company represents financial freedom. Others find it a challenge, and fail very quickly as they don't spend enough time setting up procedures and systems to make it successful in the first place. Unfortunately, passion alone is not going to cut it. So what can you do? Well, I'm sure you are sitting there reading this now and saying, but what sort of company can I set up? Well, believe it or not, my answer is it's probably right in front of you. You just can't see it yet. To find it you need to be more aware of what you are saying in conversations and try and listen out for times when you say something like "gee someone should really invent a better blah blah", or "wouldn't it be easier if you could do blah blah". These are the conversations the best ideas and businesses come from. Look, with technology being so easily accessible, perhaps the answer could be to set up something online. I believe we have only just begun to see the real power of the web, and with 5G here there's much more to be developed. I truly believe there are many more earning opportunities yet to be discovered.

Let me share something with you. Remember the <www.budgetblitz.com.au> website I mentioned a few chapters back? This is where I generate a steady cash flow twenty-four hours a day seven days a week. Sure, there was a bit of work in setting it up and I have to maintain it, but it provides me with an income from the 28 Day Budget Blitz. Obviously not much at $19.95 (less my expenses), but I don't just get a small incremental income stream, I'm also helping others to be better off.

I also have other sources of income, such as my books, my consulting, my board fees and the income I receive from my investments.

The lesson here is perhaps you too can find or create a small business opportunity that will provide you with a residual or ongoing income. Keep on thinking and then act on it.

Another great way to earn a passive income is to join a network marketing group. This is just like setting up your own company, except here you are using the systems and support network that have been developed and refined over many years. You can earn a very good income this way, but it does require you to work hard. Far too many people join for all the wrong reasons and expect to make millions straight away. Not all networking opportunities fit everyone, so do your research very carefully. And don't be pressured into it. This is a business and you should do what is called due diligence on the company you're about to hook up with. If you are not comfortable, go elsewhere. If you like them, join and learn as much as you can. Ask the successful ones to give you their tips to success. I know a number of people who have made millions this way and they are still actively involved after many years. Why you ask? Because they love it! Now that's financial freedom.

4. PROTECT WHAT YOU'VE GOT

Here's a question. Put your hand up (metaphorically not physically) if you have some or all of the following insurances: house, contents, car, boat and travel. Keep it up if you have life insurance. Okay, keep it up if you have income protection insurance. Now here's a curve ball for those who still have their hands up – keep it there if you have trauma cover and death and total and permanent disablement cover. Chances are that close to 70 per cent of those reading this book would have dropped their hands pretty much straight after life insurance. So my question continues: are you in that 70 per cent? You might say, sure Greg, I've got life insurance through my super so that should cover me. My response to that would be that you need to check the amount you are covered for to see if it's enough to pay out all of your debts, provide an income for your family for a few years and perhaps pay for your children's education. Let's face it, in this day and age the standard life cover of approximately $250,000 is just not going to be enough. It may, however, be plenty enough if you are single and have no mortgage. But it will be miles off if you've got major debts, a partner and perhaps even some kids. I can guarantee the amount you'll need will be much more than $250,000.

Think about it for a moment. You can have passive income streams and enjoy financial freedom, but if you pop off the perch and have substantial debts your partner will have to find the money to pay back the loans. That's why you always need to have the right life insurance cover. If you don't have enough, let me suggest that you take the responsibility and get it upgraded now before it's too late.

Speaking of being too late, a financial planning colleague of mine recently told me this story. If it doesn't prompt you into doing something nothing will. A few months back he got a call from his mate, a local accountant, who asked him as a favour to backdate a life insurance application, because one of his best clients had died suddenly and had no life insurance policy in place. When the client died he had a massive mortgage, huge credit card debts, a wife, two kids and a highly geared investment property. Unfortunately it was too late (and of course it is illegal to backdate a life insurance policy as my colleague quickly pointed out) and the family was going to have to sell and rent because they had so much debt it equalled the value of all their assets. It was an absolutely devastating blow to the family he left behind. As you can see, life insurance is an absolute must.

While I'm on the topic of insurances, I like to mention a few others that you really need to be properly protected. I know many people think it's a waste of money, but with examples like the one you just read you can see they are necessary. The first is trauma insurance (which gives you a lump sum payout immediately if you have a heart attack, stroke or you are diagnosed with cancer or other serious illnesses). This type of insurance has been available for almost ten years, however it has become increasingly popular in recent times due to the escalating costs associated with quality health care. Your passive income can only cover you for so much, especially if you are being hit with a lot of extra medical bills. The second insurance is total and permanent disability (TPD) insurance. This will give you a lump sum payout if you are permanently disabled and never able to work again as a result of an accident or illness.

To me, both these insurances are absolutely necessary. The premiums may cost a bit, but they are only a fraction of what you'd have to come up with if something should happen. One way to save on premiums is to consider including them under your superannuation policy, especially for TPD and life insurance.

The third insurance is one you absolutely, positively cannot be without. It's called income protection insurance, and it protects your most important asset – your capacity to earn. Imagine you are at your friends place on the weekend having a few quiet ones at a barbeque, and you slip down their back steps and break both your arms (don't laugh, this happens!). How are you going to earn your salary? Sure you may be able to take all your accrued leave, but what then? Will your boss be kind and give you paid leave? What if you are self-employed? Where's the money going to come from? Workers compensation is not going to cover any of this as it didn't happen at work. Then again, you could always sue your friend, but chances are they won't have any public risk insurance. Plus, it's probably not good form if you want to get invited back for their next barbeque. Get my point? That's why you need income protection insurance. I admit it isn't cheap, but it is tax deductible (and like most insurances, you can pay monthly). What's more it's very flexible in its set-up, which means that you can determine how long you want the waiting period before you get your payment and for how long you receive your benefit. These two factors, plus a few others, will determine your premium.

When I was crook I can't begin to tell you how secure I felt knowing I had income protection insurance. Although I didn't end up using it, I knew I had an income stream up my sleeve that I could always fall back on. After reading all of this, I hope if you make a point of topping up what you've got or going out and getting these insurances.

5. ENJOY YOURSELF

I hope by now you appreciate that insuring yourself is an absolute must, as not only will it protect you and your loved ones financially, it will give you peace of mind and enable you to get on with life and enjoy yourself.

Speaking of enjoying yourself, you need to give yourself permission to have fun. Especially if you've spent quite a long time in the pay-to-pay cycle. Celebrate each and every little win, and perhaps treat yourself (or your significant other or family) to something special for achieving one of your goals or a specific action item. (remember Chapter 2?).

Don't go overboard and relax too much, or you may land right back in the pay-to-pay cycle.

My mother's sister is a great example here. She and her husband started out very poor and lived from pay to pay. In fact, there were times when there was no pay while my uncle was building up his company. One thing about them, however, is that they used to treat themselves every time they got a new client. Not with expensive champagne or an extravagant night out, but with a sensational home-cooked meal they would prepare together. They would enjoy some wine with the meal and talk on into the night.

Over the years, as my uncle's company grew, they still followed the same tradition. The only difference being they developed a taste for lobster (bought from the fish market and cooked themselves).

Ultimately, he became financially free and was able to do whatever he liked, whenever he liked (not bad for a man who came to Australia with five pounds in his pocket and the clothes on his back).

He had a tough life; he had a good life. And he knew how to enjoy both.

I can understand that this whole area of insurance is confusing, so I always recommend you have a chat to an insurance expert.

TIME TO MAKE FINANCIAL FREEDOM HAPPEN

As I've spoken about in this chapter, when you're financially free you choose what time you get up in the morning, what activities you do, what work you do and how you have fun. Now I'm not talking retirement here, I'm talking about becoming financially free before you reach sixty, sixty-five or seventy.

Unfortunately, the majority of people across Australia who are heading for retirement are in for the shock of their life. Their biggest single asset is their house, and with a national average value of $691,000 and contents of $47,000, plus an average superannuation holding of $106,000 for men and $70,000 for women (as at Nov 2019), they simply will not have the dollars to live the life they are accustomed to.

If your goal is to live in the lap of luxury, you may have your work cut out for you, as you'll have to generate sufficient cash to first buy the assets you want and then give you a cash flow that's greater than your wage from work. If, on the other hand, your goal is to simply quit work when you want and live a normal life, then the pressure may not be as great. Either way you'll need to set up your plans now so that you can develop an ongoing passive income stream.

With the pay-to-pay cycle hopefully well and truly behind you, your next step is to set a course for your financial freedom. I've given you the tools; now it's up to you to call up that same focus, energy and discipline that got you out of the pay-to-pay cycle.

CHAPTER 7
HOW TO STAY FOCUSED

Unfortunately, there are two factors that can upset your path out of the pay-to-pay cycle.

The first deals with uncontrollable events that happen in your life, also known as the Money Monsters. These have a habit of creeping up on you and knocking your finances for a six.

The second deals with the seven deadly sins in life (greed, gluttony, lust, and so on) and how they affect your day to day finances. You'll find out more about these in a few minutes, but first I want to have a chat about the importance of your mindset in keeping focused.

Look, things happen which really make you question everything and, in fact, can make you quite depressed. I know; I've experienced it. Left unchecked you can easily spiral downwards mentally, and before you know it you could be worse off than where you started. What you need is to have a very good appreciation of the three key words I keep on mumbling about throughout this book: Focus, Energy and Discipline.

Without all of them working at the same time, you will struggle. That's why I keep on saying them over and over to get you into the mindset. My granddad was the epitome of Focus, Energy and Discipline. He came to Australia as a refugee with three kids, a wife and absolutely nothing in his pocket (at least my uncle had five pounds!). Not being able to speak English, he was sent to work in a factory whilst his wife and kids were sent to a dusty refugee camp in Bathurst, NSW.

For the next thirty years that man carved out a fantastic existence for himself and his family and never did he once complain or cause a fuss. He had a goal to make a happy and healthy life in this country and that's exactly what he did. Sure, he had his Money Monsters and deadly sins to contend with, but he dealt with them in such a positive way that he always came out with a smile on his face.

A positive mindset, and knowing the alternatives, are the keys to overcoming these obstacles. The sooner you embrace this the easier it will be for you to cope.

Speaking of coping, in this chapter I'll also share with you my simple but very effective method of keeping on top of your bills so that there are no surprises. Plus, I'll have a bit of a chat about where you can go to get a helping hand in keeping focused.

Okay. Be afraid, very afraid ... You're about to meet the dreaded Money Monsters that play havoc with your finances. As you will see, they can be daunting. But there are always ways out, especially if you have built yourself a solid emergency cash fund setup (remember Chapter 6?). If you have this fund properly stocked (with a good amount of cash, say a few thousand) you will be able to handle the following monsters more easily.

THE 7 MONEY MONSTERS

1. REDUNDANCY

A very ugly word, especially when you are hearing it in the same sentence as your name. In most circumstances redundancies come as a complete shock and can cause a pretty destabilising effect on both your confidence and, of course, your finances. I've got to say it was quite depressing when I was called into the Human Resources Manager's office and told that I wasn't needed any longer, despite the fact they thought I was a model employee. It was quite a weird feeling, as all the hard work, dedication and loyalty I'd put in suddenly seemed in vain. Anyway, you can feel sorry for yourself for a few moments but then you must go on. Remind yourself that it happens and you are going to be better off somewhere else. COVID-19 has landed many people redundant, through no fault of their own.

Now let's get to the money side of things. If you are still in the pay-to-pay cycle this may have a devastating blow to you. What you need to do is to take it calmly and focus on how you allocate your money for debts and basic needs like food, clothing and shelter. If you were lucky enough to get a lump sum and you have debts, see if you can put a great deal of that payment toward paying them off.

If you quickly get a new job (although tougher in COVID-19 times) then consider the extra payments to your debts as an accelerator (as I spoke about in Chapter 5). Then keep a bit for your normal day-to-day expenses and for some emergency money.

If you didn't get a lump sum, my suggestion is you contact your lending institutions as soon as you are made redundant and tell them what happened – see if you can get a repayment holiday. Most good lenders will give a few months grace (especially during COVID-19) as they prefer you come early and explain your situation rather than having to chase you.

If, on the other hand, you are just out of the pay-to-pay cycle and you are made redundant, you will need to follow all the recommendations I've just given plus use the emergency fund money we talked about in Chapter 6 wisely.

Believe it or not, a redundancy may be the best thing that ever happens to you. I know that may sound crazy, but think of it as an opportunity for you to perhaps re-address your career or in fact to take the "leap of faith" and start your own venture. Sure, it can be devastating, but you must always see opportunity, even in seemingly bad times.

A good friend of mine who was recently made redundant, not once but four times in one year, is a great example of this. It was not through any fault of her own, just a series of bad luck. As a very employable person she always managed to land herself a new job within a week or two of being made redundant, so any lump sum she received she banked in her Investment Account to use as capital to start up the company she had always planned. After four times she was made redundant again! This time she decided it was the gods telling her to use this as an opportunity to take a "leap of faith" and set up her own business. (I can totally relate to that!)

To do this she had to go back to study and get the appropriate qualifications. This course was an eighteen-week full-time program and meant she could only get part-time work in the meantime to pay for the bills. At only one stage did she ever to dip into her savings; for the most part she cleverly and realistically re-budgeted her expenses according to her reduced income. A very wise move.

If you are wondering how she went. Well, she passed the course with flying colours and she's now in the process of celebrating her first year in business. Her passion and good business sense are keeping her going and, as she says, "No-one can make me redundant now!"

2. SICKNESS AND ACCIDENTS

My dad always used to say "I can't afford to get sick". You know what? He never did. I don't know how he did it. Perhaps he was so focused on his business he literally willed himself into never getting sick, or maybe he was just lucky. Who knows? But the fact remains he has always been blessed with good health, even to this day.

Unfortunately, not all of us are like that, and some people are obviously much worse off. And, the one common denominator when you are sick, is it costs you money, both from the loss of income (if you are self-employed or run out of sick days at work) and from the cost of medical care.

Luckily, in Australia we are fortunate to have a great public health system. However, it only goes so far. If you want extra services or your preferential treatment, you'll have to take out private health insurance. I'm not too sure what your thoughts are about private health insurance, but I believe it is an absolute necessity (especially once you have children). Sure, it costs, but you can always claim the tax rebate and, like all the insurances I spoke about in Chapter 6, you need to protect your wealth via insurances.

Speaking about wealth, I have a saying: "Your health is your wealth". I can speak from first-hand experience here.

As you know, when I was sick, I was in the depths of the pay-to-pay cycle. But I was doing everything I could to climb out of it. However, when you are sick just thinking straight is an achievement. That's why without your health you have no capacity to earn. And with debts and expenses, you will not find yourself in a good position. That's why you need insurance to protect your income streams when you are sick, and you need private health insurance to get you back on the road faster. It may cost a bit extra, but you will not have to wait in what can be awfully long public health queues.

When I was first rushed to hospital I was admitted as a public patient (those professionals at Royal North Shore Hospital in Sydney are just something else – I can't thank them enough). When it looked like I needed extra treatment, and fast, I was rushed through the public system (with the top registrars caring for me). But then I needed more specialist help, for which I had to use my private health insurance cover.

These specialists got me back on my feet quickly. Yes, I had to pay a premium and a small gap fee, but getting my health back was the only thing on my mind. I would have paid anything for that. I'm sure if you've ever been in a similar situation you appreciate what I'm saying.

Accidents are yet another Money Monster that can cause a real financial headache (excuse the pun). Whether they involve a car crash, falling over on the street or injuring yourself in your own home, it will cost you money. Even though you may be insured for, say, a car crash, you may have to fork out some cash for the excess. Then again, if you don't have insurance it can be a whole new ball game, as it could set you into a serious tail spin. That's why your emergency money comes in so handy. It can cover the shortfall and prevent you from falling into the dreaded pay-to-pay cycle.

3. RELATIONSHIPS

American comedian Rita Rudner cheekily sums up what tends to happen when it comes to relationships and money. "I love to shop after a bad relationship. I don't know why. I buy a new outfit and it makes me feel better. It just does. And sometimes if I see a really great outfit, I'll break up with someone on purpose."

For her it seems that her Therapist spending mindset takes over both when she's sad and when she's happy. In fact, this tends to happen to all of us when we start and finish relationships. Think about it for a moment: ask yourself how much money you spent in your life when you started a new relationship. Then think about how much you spent when it ended. For some this may not be much, but for others it could be massive (divorce settlements!). Either way, if you were (or are still) in the pay-to-pay cycle, relationships could have a big impact.

Clearly there are more stages to a relationship than a beginning and an end. In fact, I think there are nine, and each one has a different impact on your finances. These stages will be different for everyone, as they can take a week, a year, ten years or a lifetime to cycle through. But what remains constant is the fact they will make some sort of impact.

3. HOW THE NINE STAGES IN A RELATIONSHIP AFFECT YOUR FINANCES

Let me show you what I mean. In the first stage, which I like to call "The Catch", you generally find yourself searching for the love of your life! This could involve going to friends' barbeques, pubs and clubs, and swiping on Tinder or Grindr or whatever dating app you prefer.

If you successfully strike up a conversation, it may lead to a drink or a coffee. However, if nothing happens after this you start again and repeat until you find someone you click with. This could get expensive over a long period of time.

If, however, there is a connection, you may get the opportunity to set up a "date". From here the relationship moves into stage two, the "Courtship" phase. In this stage both individuals end up spending a fair bit as the first date may involve a fancy restaurant and expensive drinks. Both may also buy new clothes to make a good impression.

Again, this can really blow out the budget if you get carried away. Think about it. If, after a few dates going to fancy restaurants (and doing things you normally wouldn't do, like hot air ballooning or going to the opera!) and hours of conversation, things might be looking good and the relationship moves into the third stage.

This is the "Romance" phase. Here, your casual dating becomes much more formal and you start to see a lot more of each other. Your spending is still high, as you now start going on mini-breaks away where you stay in nice places and maybe eat out a lot. Now this is a real danger period for your finances, as in the bliss of a blossoming relationship you can become blasé and whack everything on the old credit card without worrying about the mounting debts.

I know this period of a relationship is just great, but it can really damage the good work you have done to get yourself out of the pay-to-pay cycle. The trick here is to date someone rich and have them pay ... just kidding. Seriously, you just need to have a quiet moment and perhaps re-plan your money, or suggest less money hungry activities.

And that brings me to stage four. The "Commitment" phase. Here, things really start becoming serious. Perhaps you both decide to move in together to save on rent, or even decide to buy a place together (either way, this is going to affect your money). Moving in together will definitely save money. However, if you both continue to go out and party on the cash left over, there's no real financial gain. This phase may even involve a wedding, which will create a whole new set of expenses that you may or may not have expected.

You are probably thinking that you can't put a value on a relationship – I agree with that. But you can and should spend time together discussing your money. Otherwise, you could end up back in the pay-to-pay cycle yourself or, worse still, drag your new partner right back down there with you.

The fifth stage is the "Honeymoon" phase. Here, your expenditure slows a little as you start eating more home-cooked dinners. On the other hand, if you have just bought a place to live or moved house you'll probably be up for a few extra bucks for redecorating or renovating, both of which are fraught with potential problems which can send your finances into a real spin (read about these domestic blow-ups in a few minutes).

Speaking of blow-ups, the sixth stage is the beginning of a potential downward spiral in your relationship. Although it is not the end, it is called the "Rude Awakening" phase, because it generally involves you or your partner starting to see things about each other you didn't see before as you were blinded by your blissful emotions. Sooner or later little issues bubble to the top, especially if you are both completely different money personalities. Unfortunately, too many relationships fall apart because of money problems. This can be avoided if you simply understand and appreciate each other's money personality.

The seventh stage is called the "Remorse" phase. (Yes, I'm being a bit dramatic.) It generally involves the questioning of the overall relationship, probably triggered by a prolonged breakdown in communications. The words "loneliness" and "boredom" come to mind. It is as if you have run out of conversation with the other person. As a coping mechanism, the Therapist Spender mindset subconsciously kicks in for some people as it clearly helps overcome the loneliness and boredom. Not good for the relationship, and definitely not good for your credit card or savings account either.

Left unchecked, this remorse quickly turns into the eighth stage – "The Crossroads". Here is where the relationship can go either one way or another. Whichever way it goes it is going to cost you money, potentially destabilising your finances. Let's say you agree to try and make things right again. You'll probably spend a heap of money going away for a weekend escape or sending flowers, neither of which are sustainable long-term solutions. If your relationship is in serious decline, you need to seek professional help. This again will cost you, but you need to weigh up the importance of keeping or losing your relationship – so cost shouldn't come into it.

Speaking of losing your relationship, this brings me to the last stage. It's the "Rest a Bit" phase, where you both agree to either live separately (costing you money) or to separate totally (again costing you in cash or in assets such as the house and your super being split). Unfortunately, this part of the cycle can end quite messily and cost you a fortune in re-establishing yourself again (and possibly in legal fees). Been there, done that my ex-finance from many years back who effectively leaving without a trace and taking all the furniture and fittings. This left me with no other choice than to go out and buy a whole apartment's worth of furniture! $20,000 later I had replaced everything! Not happy!

I'm sure you've probably gone through many of these stages and can relate to them in some way. The key message from all of them is to try and control your emotions when it comes to finances. I know it's very hard to do, but if you want to protect yourself from slipping back into that pay-to-pay cycle you are going to have to think twice about how you spend and manage your money in a relationship. An appreciation of your partner's money personality plus open communication can go a very long way to domestic bliss!

4. DOMESTIC BREAK UPS

Speaking of domestic bliss, this can easily turn into a living nightmare when things around the home either blow up, stop working or break down. Don't you just hate it when one of your appliances goes on the blink and the others somehow know and go out in "sympathy"! It seems there is some unwritten law: whenever one thing goes bung, another one or two follow.

What you are left with is the prospect of forking out big bucks in repair bills or buying something new. It can be extremely frustrating when you just get back on top of your finances and you experience a domestic break-up. You know what I'm talking about here; things like your car needing expensive repairs, the back fence falling down, the house being damaged in a storm, the pets getting sick, your fridge, washing machine or vacuum cleaner giving up the ghost. These things can cost thousands.

Coping with these domestic break-ups are a real challenge as they can deliver devastating blows to your finances – especially if you are in the pay-to-pay cycle. The key is to be prepared and have things like pet insurance (see <www.rspcapetinsurance.org.au>), the right amount of home insurance, the ability to shop smart to get the bargain replacements (at seconds stores, auctions and eBay, etc) and, ultimately, an Emergency Savings account to help you through these little glitches.

When it comes to things like home insurance, more than 70 per cent of people are under-insured by a factor of 10 per cent. Doesn't sound much, but if your home burns to the ground or is severely damaged by a storm you could be out of pocket by thousands.

Your best bet is to talk to your insurance company and ask for their opinion, seek professional builders, or contact someone like Archicentre (The Royal Institute for Architects) <www.archicentre.com.au> to help you get an estimate of building costs.

5. DEATH AND TAXES

As the saying goes, there are only two certainties in life: death and taxes. While you normally can't predict when you are going to die, you can certainly prepare for it so that your loved ones won't be left out of pocket. I covered life insurance in Chapter 6, so hopefully by now you are convinced that you need it or have to top it up. But there are two other things you can do to make it as easy as possible for your loved ones.

The first is to have a will. A will sets out how you want your assets and other personal matters distributed, and the reason you need one is, even if you don't have loved ones, you will still have some money coming from your super fund and perhaps your attached life insurance policy. If you die without a valid will, you will be what they call intestate, which means that a government department will administer the distribution of your assets. Think about it. If you actually did have dependants and died intestate it could take literally months for the government department to unravel your money and other assets.

While I'm on the topic of wills, I'd like to point out that you need to also keep them updated to reflect any major changes in your life – get married or divorced, have children and so on. This way, those who you want to get your money will get it without a massive money grab between people after you're gone!

The second area you can plan is to pre-pay for your funeral costs (this should be covered in your life insurance policy). According to Choice Magazine, the average cost of a funeral ranges from $4,000 to $15,000. This can be a major cash drain when you are either in or just about to break free of the pay-to-pay cycle. Coping with a death in the family is hard enough; that's why having an updated will in place and a pre-paid funeral will take away a great deal of pressure both emotionally and financially. I know it's spooky stuff but it's necessary. Unfortunately, death is part of life.

The other side of the certainties are taxes, and one of your main objectives is to claim all the appropriate deductions you can so as to pay as little tax as possible. This way you will have a better cash flow which may help you get out of the pay-to-pay cycle faster or let you add to some of your investment savings money if you are out of the cycle. One thing to make sure of is that your tax avoidance activities are legal – not tax evasion. Tax evasion, my friend, is very illegal. Let's say you haven't put a tax return in for a few years and probably owe the Australian Tax Office some money. My recommendation is to talk to a tax accountant first and seek their advice on how to best approach the tax department and report your plight. Just like the banks, tax department would like to hear from you early if you owe them money. They also appreciate your honesty and will be open to negotiate a better payback arrangement of any fines you owe.

Speaking of fines, these are another thing that can catch you out. Nowadays, particularly in the cities, parking fines seem to be issued freely. There's nothing more frustrating than receiving a fine on your windscreen. I can only suggest you try and avoid them, but if you get hit pay it when it comes in (well, wait until you get the reminder notice at least) and be done with it.

Other traffic infringements can also cause a huge hit to the budget, especially if you break the road rules during the double demerit holiday periods. I'm not going to tell you what to do, but remember, it is only a matter of time before you get caught if you are a serial speeder or you talk on your phone while driving – and it is going to cost you dearly. Think about it: a $300 fine to State Government could have gone a long way to paying off a credit card!

6. THE UNEXPECTED CHILD

Did you know, according to the National Centre for Social and Economic Modelling, it costs the average family (and note the word average!) at least $406,000 to raise a child from birth to the age of twenty. For two kids that's $812,000. That's almost a million for raising kids!

Crikey, how much is a packet of condoms?

Seriously, though, this brings a whole new perspective to the cost of having a family. The bottom line is that a child costs big money to bring into this world and no matter what part of the pay-to-pay cycle journey you are on, having an unexpected child could catastrophically change your finances forever. Let's face it, you've got to effectively take responsibility for the life of another human being for about twenty years.

During that time you will not only have to feed your child, you will also have to educate them. Schooling costs are not cheap and can set you back anywhere from $1,000 to $20,000 per year in fees alone. Not to mention the costs of simply getting your child back to school each year (around $2000 per child).

I'm not here to give you a lecture on family planning, nor am I saying you should view having children as a pure economic decision. Far from it. What I am talking about is that it does cost money to have kids, and I'm suggesting that you plan as best you can. If you are thinking of having children, perhaps you can consider starting by renaming one of your savings accounts (remember Chapter 6) to, for example, an account called "I'm having a child account".

Just like you'd do anyway, put some money away each week. This money will come in handy when your child is born and, if you continue to contribute, will also come in handy for school fees and education.

I've done this myself for my two boys. As soon as we found out we were expecting I started a separate high interest savings account. I set up an auto deduction from another saving account of mine and also gave out the account details to their grandparents, who wanted to contribute on an ongoing basis. My oldest son, who turns ten in 2020, now has $15,000 to his name. Although he is not able to touch it yet; it will be given to him when he is 18.

If you are interested in saving for your child's education and want a more formal savings product, there are many education funds available that have been set up specifically for parents (and grandparents) to invest in.

Before I move on to the next point, I'd like to share with you a quick story of what happened during a presentation I gave a few years ago. It will definitely bring a smile to your face, but at the same time bring home an important point. Back when I used to be on a radio station in Sydney we would do outside broadcasts; sometimes I'd get up after the broadcast and have a chat to the audience that was sitting around the outside broadcast booth.

One day I thought I'd talk about money personalities, so I asked a twenty-something bloke from the audience to come up on stage with me so that we could discover what sort of money personality he had. As sort of a party trick, I can tell a person's Money Personality by the look and contents of their wallet! Now, this bloke's wallet was pretty good on the outside as it looked well-kept and clean. On the inside, he had his driver's licence, Medicare card, uni card, debit card, $50 cash and a few coins. I don't think he was expecting me to take out all the contents one by one and show them to the audience, but I think he got the shock of his life when I pulled out a condom from a side pocket.

As you can imagine, the whole audience erupted with laughter. Rather than make him embarrassed I quickly said to the audience that he was in fact doing two very smart things by carrying the condom around. First, he'd be protecting his health; second, he'd be protecting himself against being pinned down in the pay-to-pay cycle by an unexpected twenty-year expenditure of $406,000 (the total cost of raising a child). Want to know what his money personality turned out to be? Careful!

7. FRAUD

More and more people are falling prey to sophisticated scams, and this is an easy way for you to lose your hard-earned savings. To me there are two main areas of fraud:

I. THE IDENTITY THIEF

Phishing scams are happening constantly, and scammers are becoming more and more sophisticated every day. All they need is to get things like your credit card number and expiry date, your driver's licence number, your bank BSB and account numbers or your date of birth and they are away. According to the ABS 1.6 million Australians aged over fifteen were a victim of personal fraud with a total $3 billion.

The way to beat this is to not throw away your bank statements, shred any documentation that contains your personal information and never respond to an email that says it is from your bank and is requesting your password. Some important information you need to know about identity theft is that you won't get your money back from unauthorised transactions if you acted fraudulently or didn't keep your PIN or password secret (think about that one!). The same goes if you unreasonably delay telling your account institution that your card has been lost or stolen or that someone else may know your PIN or code. The moral to the story: keep PINs secure, and if anything happens call immediately, even if you lose your wallet for a few minutes.

II. GET RICH QUICK SCHEMES

These make my blood boil. Every year thousands of people go along to seminars about options and futures trading or property investment with the hope of finding that magical answer. Unfortunately, many of them don't have two dollars to their name, or any detailed knowledge about sophisticated investment strategies.

All are lured by the potential of making heaps of money, and the only people who make the money in the end are the seminar organisers, who rip off these unsuspecting folk. Many of them should be attending workshops on getting the basics right, but that's not as sexy as the promise of making millions, is it? My recommendation here is, if you're considering going to a seminar, do your homework first and think about why you need to go in the first place and what benefits you'll get out of it. Plus, have a look at who's presenting. If you've never heard of them go onto the ASIC website <www.asic.gov.au> and do a search for their name. You may be surprised what you find.

THE 7 DEADLY SELF-INFLICTED MONEY SINS

You thought Money Monsters were bad? Hold onto your hats. You're about to discover an even scarier set of things that can cause you to lose focus and fall right back into the pay-to-pay cycle. I call them, the 7 Deadly Self-Inflicted Money Sins, and they are based on the old seven deadly sins of sloth, gluttony, envy, anger, lust, pride and greed. How do they affect your money, you ask?

Well, let me explain.

1. SLOTH

If you are still finding yourself saying that "this money stuff is too boring", "I'll get to those bills next week" or "I'll have a look for a better deal for my credit cards soon", put down this book now and say out loud: "I am a loser!"

Sorry to be so harsh, but I want to jolt you into action. It's your life and it's your money, so make the most of it. Being lazy or not having enough time is no excuse. You have to make the effort. Let's face it, if you are consistently late with your bills or your repayments (generally greater than ninety days) you could end up with a black mark on your credit record or paying late payment fees, which is a very bad use of your hard-earned money.

A black mark on your credit record will definitely affect your ability to get a mortgage or a personal loan and, of course, the interest rate you pay if you do find a lender who is prepared to lend to you.

By the way, if you want to see what's on your credit file hop onto <www.mycreditfile.com.au> and request a copy. It is well worth checking out as sometimes there are things put there by mistake. It would be better to find them now and fix them, rather than later when you are applying for some sort of credit and being declined.

To overcome sloth, you simply need to apply the three words that I've been banging on about all through this book – focus, energy and discipline. The world is not going to come to you nor will your finances be magically fixed overnight (well, you might win the lottery or marry rich!).

In reality, you have to work at it and keep yourself focused on achieving the goals you set in Chapter 2. Having them gives you clarity and hope. Just add a bit of energy and discipline and the sloth bug will disappear. If, however, you do find yourself getting a bit complacent, you should turn to a friend or anyone in your money team (your mortgage broker, solicitor, financial planner, etc) for some reassurance or guidance.

2. GLUTTONY

The sin du jour! As I have mentioned time and again in this book, we are all falling prey to the "got to have it now" bug. As a consequence, we are spending 150 per cent of our income (remember Chapter 4 when I spoke about the income to expense ratio?). If our voracious appetite for spending continues, we'll be in real strife. Perhaps you need to be a bit like my mum and think twice before you buy something new.

COVID-19 or no COVID-19, next time you are standing in front of all those sexy electronic gadgets or flat screen TVs with surround sound, ask yourself the question: "Is this a need or a want?" If that's not working for you and you are then still under the influence of the "got to have it now bug", do the old "divide your hourly wage rate by the total price of what you are buying" trick. In other words, this assumes that if you did nothing else with your hourly pay, it would take you a certain number of hours of work to cover the cost of that item.

Let me tell you about a real example of one of my friends who has the classic "Drunken Sailor" mindset. She just can't help herself spending and has literally more than 100 pairs of shoes. Each of them is probably worth $200; that's around $20,000 in shoes alone. No wonder she has nothing to show for years of working. One day we were out shopping and she wanted to buy a $350 pair of shoes (you can imagine my reaction). I contained myself and got her to divide the cost of the shoes by her hourly wage rate. Given that she was earning $32 an hour and the shoes were $350 she would have to work nearly 11 hours (well over a day and a bit) just to afford these shoes. At first she said to me in quite a nonchalant voice "Oh, that's nothing", but when I reminded her that her whole salary for a day and a bit was now only to be used for the purchase of her shoes – not food, rent and a bus ticket – she quickly changed her mind. The result: she bought a $50 pair of sandals instead.

3. ENVY

"Forget what others have got and just focus on what you want and need" were the words of my mum when I was a growing up. She did her very best to instil these values in me when I'd come home from a mate's place and say how brilliant their house was as they had a colour TV and we didn't. (Yikes, this really shows you how old I am.)

Clearly, envy is about wanting something others have, and in this "got to have it now society" it often leads to a ridiculous spending spree just to be seen to be equal in material things. A subculture of neighbourly competition is becoming the norm, and is pushing up spending on want-related items. A classic example of this is a mate of my brother, who lives in a street where all the neighbours have an unspoken competition to have the biggest and best Christmas lights on their home each year. So much so that some of them are spending up to $3,000 a year on newer and more impressive systems. That's $3,000 that could go toward their child's education, the mortgage or future investment. Envy is an expensive business; those who fall prey to it, especially those just out of the pay-to-pay cycle, will be the first to really hurt when the boom times slow.

4. ANGER

Getting cranky is never going to make things happen in a positive way. If you always think negative, negative things will happen. On the contrary, think positive and positive things will happen. This is where quantum physics comes in. Check it out, it is fascinating. Essentially, the theory is our beliefs about reality can affect that reality so that it fits our perspective. So get those positive thoughts out to the universe (write down goals and maybe even have some visual stimulus, like a clipping from a magazine of a house you want to own one day). Convince yourself every day that you will achieve your goals. Sooner or later it will happen.

I wish I could tell you how it works but I have been following this for some time now and really believe that if you are a positive person you attract positive things. People will come into your life for certain purposes. In some cases you won't realise why until later, but ultimately that interaction will be a positive one contributing to the achievement of one of your goals. Sounds new age, but we need to remove ourselves from our traditional two dimensions of money (we have it or not) and use our energy to give us what we want.

Anger can stop you from doing this. Don't blame others for your situation. Take responsibility and find better ways. Use your connections and harness your energy. Your anger will simply disappear. If you are shaking your head with disbelief now, chances are you are still in the pay-to-pay cycle. The essence is not to be angry when you get unexpected bills or bank fees, but to be more focused on finding better solutions by using your positive energy to get better deals.

5. LUST

A necessary evil when it comes to relationships, but don't let it take over your wallet. In the Courtship and Romance stages I mentioned before you need to temper your spending on things like new clothes and eating out. Exert a bit of self-restraint (or call it discipline) to keep your spending under control, as your emotions can really get away from you and bring out the Therapist Spender mindset. Enough said.

6. PRIDE

Are you living a champagne lifestyle on a beer budget? If you are, then you'll need to go back and re-read this book. If not, I hope you have started to make the necessary changes to bring it back to a more practical ($15 bottle of wine) budget! For example, if you are living in a place that you simply can't afford, you need to move to a cheaper one. Also, if you have a car that you don't really need, sell it and buy a cheaper one, or catch public transport for a while. Sure, it may hurt your pride to do these things, but it may be a better solution than being declared bankrupt.

If your friends think less of you for doing this, you may need to reassess your friends. Remember, while friends can come and go, debts have a habit of becoming lifelong companions. Making a few changes for a longer-term gain (I call this pruning for regrowth) may be tough in the short term. But if you maintain your positive attitude and follow your goals, you will get back to where you were in a shorter period than you may have first thought.

"While friends can come and go, debts have a habit of becoming lifelong companions."

Sometimes pride can be confused with image, and in this image conscious world you live in (thanks to the marketers of brands) you need to be strong and ignore all the marketing hype. Sure, it is tough to resist. But you need to remember, people selling really don't care if you are in the pay-to-pay cycle. All they want is your hard-earned money.

7. GREED

Greed is a basic human function that is inadvertently drummed into us when we are little children. In the early stages of our early development all we know is a one-way giving relationship from our parents, and this is imprinted into our personalities forever. Those who let greed take over can often get caught up in the pursuit of money and hence lose touch with what really matters (like their health and relationships).

To overcome this deadliest of money sins, you have to set your sights on first meeting your needs and then (if there is money left over) start satisfying your wants. I know it's very hard given all the temptations around offering you easy ways to acquire things using discounts, easy payment terms. But you need to resist and keep a clear focus on what you want to achieve, and that is to get out of the pay-to-pay cycle and have financial freedom.

HOW TO GET YOURSELF ORGANISED

Now that you've got a good handle on all the controllable and uncontrollable things that can prevent you from getting and staying out of the pay-to-pay cycle (Money Monsters and the deadly money sins), I thought I would share with you a set of basic things I do to keep my money paperwork under control. It is these little things that make the big differences between feeling in control of your money ... or not. Having a simple and efficient system will ensure that you will be able to pay your bills on time and get on with your normal day-to-day life. Best of all, you won't be pinged with late fees.

Before I share with you my routine, I just want to draw your attention to a survey produced for Australia Post by Newspoll, which showed that 50 per cent of all household bill payers in Australia don't know how much in total they pay each year for their electricity, gas, water, council rates and telephone. On top of this, the survey found that nearly four out of five households don't have a detailed system for paying their bills.

Rather than shoving your bills into a draw or stacking them in a pile hoping they will all go away, you need to be organised. Over the years I've developed a simple system that has served me well. There's no rocket science to it as I assure you, a simple system is often the best. Remember, money doesn't need to be complicated.

Here's a seven-step guide you can adapt to whether you prefer online bills or paper.

STEP 1. SET UP EMAIL FOLDERS OR BUY A BOX OF MANILA FOLDERS

These are your basic ingredients to getting organised. You'll see what I mean in a moment.

STEP 2. SET UP A "CURRENT BILLS" FOLDER

In this folder put all the bills that fall due in the current month. Don't worry about labelling it with anything else other than Current Bills, as once you have paid them you will be refiling them into other folders.

STEP 3. SET UP A "NEXT MONTH'S BILLS" FOLDER

If you do get a bill that is not due in the current month, put it in here as the last thing you should be doing is paying something before it is due.

STEP 4. MAKE A SEPARATE FOLDER FOR EACH OF THE FOLLOWING

A bit of work is required here as you'll need to create a few email folders or grab a few manila folders and put a number of names at the top of them. Here's a list for you to start you off, but I'm sure you've got others:

- credit card (if you have more than one card, make up a separate folder for each)
- personal loan
- home loan
- savings statements
- rates
- rent
- gas
  electricity
- water
- home phone, mobile, internet
- school fees

- day care fees
- superannuation
- dividend statements (if you own shares it is a good idea to create a separate folder for each company you own shares in)
- insurances – car, home, contents, health, income protection, warranty cards, car registration papers

STEP 5. FILE EACH BILL OR STATEMENT IN ITS APPROPRIATE FOLDER AS IT ARRIVES

Only put bills in these folders. That way you won't have a huge, depressing "money paperwork pile" to wade through at the end of the month.

STEP 6. FILE YOUR BILLS IN DATE ORDER

In all your folders put the most recent statement or bill at the front of the folder. This will be particularly handy in the current file as you will then know what's urgent.

STEP 7. STORE YOUR FOLDERS IN A SAFE PLACE

Digital filing is definitely the way to go. To store manila folders will require something like a small filing cabinet or perhaps a portable file (both are not that expensive and can sit nicely in a cupboard somewhere).

I constantly follow this process as it keeps my paperwork and ultimately my bills under control. I moved from physical folders to digital email folders as fast as I could, as to me it was so much more efficient. But, whatever works for you.

As a crosscheck, I also look back at my 12 Month Budget Planner template (remember Chapter 3) and look carefully to see if there are any changes to my bills over time. It's surprising what sort of trends you can pick up, and you sometimes spot errors in your bills. The message here is to check every bill and check it against your last to see if you have been charged properly. Again, never forget it is your money and never be embarrassed to ask for clarification, even if it turns out that the amount is correct.

All this sounds great, but you might say you just don't have time for this. Sure you are busy, but all of this only takes a couple of minutes a day and about half an hour a month. Not much for keeping your finances on track and keeping well out of the pay-to-pay cycle.

A HELPING HAND TO KEEP YOU ON TRACK

As I've mentioned a few times in the book, you can get help in all different shapes and sizes in the money world. The trick is to know who to talk to.

For me, the secret (as I mentioned in Chapter 6) is to have a money team around you that you can rely on for knowledge and assistance with all things financial. Some will cost you money just to see them, while others do the work for free. For debts you'll need a mortgage broker who can help you find the best debt structure and repayment plan. They are generally free and are a good to know.

For your tax you'll obviously need a tax accountant. You'll have to pay, but it is tax deductible. For contracts (when you buy a house, for example) you'll need a solicitor. They can charge like a wounded bull, so be careful. Before you engage a solicitor ask them how they charge and how much time they estimate it will take them. Some of them will be taken aback by this. If they are, move to another one.

For your investments, you'll need a financial planner. You will generally have to pay for their advice, but having one is something you should not be without. A good one is worth their weight in gold.

For keeping your paperwork in order you can always get a bookkeeper. This can be costly, but if that's what it takes to get your finances in order, then so be it.

If you need someone to help you set your goals, put together a budget that makes sense and get a handle on your debt and savings activities, then find a money coach. They are not financial planners as they simply help you with the basics and don't provide advice on financial investment products. But they can help you straighten out your finances so that you can then talk to a financial planner.

These professionals can often be found via recommendations from your friends, relatives and work colleagues. I definitely suggest you follow their recommendations. If you fall short, just hop onto my website <www.budgetblitz.com.au> and check out my listing of professionals. Please note, the reason I've put this on my website and not in this book is that weblinks change far too often – I don't want to be sending you on a wild goose chase when I can keep them updated constantly on the web.

One final word on the money team. If you are really in trouble and are in fear of slipping into bankruptcy, I recommend you very quickly contact a credit counsellor (I've mentioned them before in the book). Again hop onto my site and find a link to one near you. They are free and well worth your time to call. Again, don't feel embarrassed or let your pride get in the way.

A Savvy money personality (remember Chapter 1?) always surrounds themselves with a good money team. If you want to become a Savvy money person, I strongly suggest you start building one now.

AND NOW IT'S TIME FOR ME TO BID YOU A FOND FAREWELL

After many pages, templates, stories about my mum, dad, relatives and friends, I truly hope you can see that breaking out of the pay-to-pay cycle is quite a straight-forward process if you want to make a change to your life.

Sure, you can go on the way you are in your comfort zone, but living on the edge from pay to pay isn't any fun. You get used to it, but there are so many things you can do and explore once you break out. I want you to promise by saying the following out loud twice in a big loud voice (don't worry if you are sitting next to someone ... they should be getting in on the act as well): "I am going to get control of my money now and live the life I want to live". Go on, don't be shy.

When you are saying it, emphasise the words "I" and "now". See, that wasn't hard after all, was it? Now say this every morning until you are well and truly out of the pay-to-pay cycle. Say it loud and say it proud.

Of course, you can say things but you also have to do things. That's why you are going to have to put into action many of the things you've read in this book that are relevant to you. Not everything will be totally relevant, but please do yourself a favour and make the investment in this book worthwhile by doing something today. Perhaps start in Chapter 1 by finding out your money personality, before coming back in a few days and getting stuck into your goals.

Take it at your own pace; remember, there's no quick fix or magic wand (I'd be a zillionaire if I had one!). It has probably taken you years to get where you are now, and if you're in a bad situation it could take some time to rectify it. But stick with it. The key is to stay positive no matter what (it's hard, but life does go on and you have to make the best of what's in front of you). Promise me you will be focused, energised and disciplined.

I've so enjoyed writing this book and I really hope that, more importantly, you got an abundance of ideas, insights and techniques out of it.

I'll now leave you with a Chinese Proverb that pretty much sums up everything I've been talking about in this book:

When planning for a year, plant corn.
When planning for a decade, plant trees.
When planning for life, train and educate people.

Hopefully I have been able to train, educate and most importantly inspire you for now and for the rest of your life.

After all, it's your money and your life, so make the most of them both.

Goodbye for now, good luck and the best of health, wealth and happiness.

CHAPTER 8

TIME TO MAKE IT HAPPEN!

Okay you've now read the book. Time to start putting things into action. I know you're busy and things always get in the way, especially when it comes to making changes to your money life. Things seem to take ages, particularly when you get caught up in the red tape around changing things like your credit cards and loans.

I for one know how hard it is trying to keep all the balls in the air at the same time. But if you are ever going to get out of the pay-to-pay cycle, just reading a book and getting motivated is not going to get you anywhere.

It's going to take real effort.

So that you don't have any excuses I have done some of the hard stuff for you and put together an easy to follow month-by-month guide (I like to call it Your Monthly Activity Calendar) Once again, you can hop onto my website <www.budgetblitz.com.au> and download it.

You can either take it month by month (starting right now or at the beginning of the financial or calendar year) or, if you are in a hurry, you can apply most of the calendar to a twelve-week period. Either way you need to keep focused.

I can guarantee if you follow the ideas and concepts in this book, you will break out of the pay-to-pay cycle!

CHAPTER 8

YOUR MONTHLY ACTIVITY CALENDAR

Month	What to do	How to do it	Why you need to do it	Reference Chapter
1	Get a good handle on your money personality	Do the money personality diagnostic test and read up on how you can change your personality.	You need to understand what makes you tick when it comes to money. Once you discover this, you'll be able to make the necessary changes to adjust your money management habits for the better.	Chapter 1
2	Spend a number of hours really thinking about where you are going in your life and what you want to do. This is your future you are talking about so really invest the time thinking of the big picture).	Start filling out the Your Goals template and keep in mind the WAMIT formula.	You need to know where you are going, otherwise you'll keep repeating the same old things every day of your life and never get anywhere.	Chapter 2
3	Get a grip on how you pay and manage your bills.	Set up a simple filing system to get some order to your paperwork.	An organised paperwork system will enable to synchronise your bill payments with your income so that you can plan your bills better and hopefully never be late or behind again.	Chapter 7
4	Gain a good understanding on where your money is coming from and where it's going.	Spend 4 weeks tracking every cent you spend using the Money Tracker template. Or subscribe to the 28 Day Budget Blitz	If you know where the cents are going, you'll be able to easily work out what to cut back on – and be able to find up $20,000 in savings without a pay rise.	Chapter 3

Month	What to do	How to do it	Why you need to do it	Reference Chapter
5	Develop a 12-month picture of your cash flows	Put together your Budget Planner template. Yes, it may seem tedious, but this will give you a very good picture of where your income is spent across a number of categories. Use as accurate figures as you can – don't fool yourself that things are doing much better than they really are.	Things will pop out here for sure as you'll find that some months you are in the red and others you are in the black. This will give you clues on what areas to work on (e.g. instead of paying annual insurances which may destroy your cash flow in one month simply pay monthly to smooth out the burden).	Chapter 3
6	Exterminate the "got to have it now bug".	Every time you spend money ask yourself whether you really need what you're buying at the point of purchase. You need to start sharpening your understanding of what you actually need versus what you want. You may have to delay certain wants until things are looking a bit better financially.	This will help sharpen your focus between needs and wants and make you think seriously about how you spend and manage your money.	Chapter 1
7	Time to adjust your spending habits	Be smarter with the way you spend. Go back to the basics and shop with lists, compare prices and look for deals. Above all try and restrict the usage of your credit card.	Being more in tune with your spender mindset will enable you to not only improve it will give you more confidence in knowing that you are more focused on getting the best value for your hard-earned dollars.	Chapter 4

Month	What to do	How to do it	Why you need to do it	Reference Chapter
8	Start to pay yourself first	Choose from any number of savings strategies I mentioned and stick to one. Most of all start by building an emergency fund. Also spend some time analysing how you can implement the Money Allowable so that you can start to build up extra money to use to create extra cash or to use in the Debt Buster Program.	Having a little bit of savings money has great psychological benefits, and the more you have the more in control of your money you will feel.	Chapter 6
9	Give your debts a health check	Take a close look at how your debts are structured and investigate ways to reduce your payments by refinancing, consolidating, or switching cards etc. Check out various websites or call your finance provider or broker.	One of your biggest expenses is probably your debts. Get them under control and you are halfway there.	Chapter 5
10	Pay off your debts faster	Get stuck into the Debt Buster Program	This program is guaranteed to get you out of debt in much faster than you ever thought possible. The bottom line is that you'll save thousands of dollars in interest.	Chapter 5

Month	What to do	How to do it	Why you need to do it	Reference Chapter
11	Look for ways to earn more income	Earning income from one source is not a smart thing. Otherwise you will be stuck in the same cycle. You need to start looking for opportunities to earn a passive income, or see if you can sell some unwanted things around your home on eBay or Facebook to make extra cash for the short-term. You could even set up a home business (the possibilities are endless with the web). Or retrain and get a better job. You are only limited by your confidence.	Retrain your mindset to be more open to following your dreams. Don't say "one day" – make it today.	Chapter 6
12	Reset your goals for the next year	Spend a fair amount of time reflecting on what happened over the last 12 months and tick off the things you achieved. Create a list of things that got in the way and ask yourself whether they are Money Monsters or the 7 Deadly Money Sins.	Things change and so must your goals. The road out of the pay-to pay-cycle can be tough. To break free you need to be focused and have a clear picture of what you are aiming for. Ongoing revision of your goals will give you just that.	Chapter 2 and Chapter 7

CHAPTER 8

YOUR PERSONAL CONTRACT WITH ME

Time to put your money where your mouth is!

PLEASE SIGN BELOW, SCAN AND EMAIL

I want you to enter into a Personal Contract with me so that you are committed to the making the appropriate changes the next 12 months to get you out of the pay-to-pay cycle.

Tell me how you are going! Email me at info@budgetblitz.com.au or log on to the site and share your thoughts in my forum.

Dear Greg,

I understand it is up to me to:

MAKE CHANGES to my attitude to dealing with money

BELIEVE in the money outcome I want

BEHAVE differently in the way I manage my money

I .... (insert your name here) understand that changing the way I think and believe about money is a daily process I need to focus on. Therefore I hereby promise to put the above Monthly Activity Calendar into action.

Signed ....

Dated ....

Witnessed By ....

Take a photo of this page and put it on my Instagram to share.

#budgetblitz

ACKNOWLEDGEMENTS

There are so many people to thank and limited time to do so. I don't want to bore the socks off the audience by rattling off lists of names.

I promise I'll be short and sweet, but please indulge me for at least the next sixty seconds.

To my family, friends and work colleagues, thank you for the inspiration. You have no idea how often you triggered ideas in my head with the normal day-to-day conversations we have had. For that I thank you.

Finally, I'd like to thank you for buying this book. Through your support I can continue to create books like this to help others better understand money, become more confident with it and ultimately enjoy their lives without the pressure of money woes.